EARTH'S JOURNEY
INTO HOPE

The Orbis Series on Integral Ecology publishes books seeking to integrate an understanding of Earth's interconnected life systems with sustainable social, political, and economic systems that enhance the Earth community. Books in the series concentrate on ways to

- Reexamine human–Earth relations in light of contemporary cosmological and ecological science
- Develop visions of common life marked by ecological integrity and social justice
- Expand on the work of those exploring such fields as integral ecology, climate justice, Earth law, ecofeminism, and animal protection
- Promote inclusive participatory strategies that enhance the struggle of Earth's poor and oppressed for ecological justice
- Deepen appreciation for dialogue within and among religious traditions on issues of ecology and justice
- Encourage spiritual discipline, social engagement, and the transformation of religion and society toward these ends

Viewing the present moment as a time for fresh creativity and inspired by the encyclical *Laudato si'*, the series seeks authors who speak to ecojustice concerns and who bring into this dialogue perspectives from the Christian communities, from the world's religions, from secular and scientific circles, or from new paradigms of thought and action.

ECOLOGY & JUSTICE SERIES

EARTH'S JOURNEY INTO HOPE

Reflections on Thomas Berry's Great Work

BRIAN EDWARD BROWN

ORBIS BOOKS

Maryknoll, New York 10545

Founded in 1970, Orbis Books endeavors to publish works that enlighten the mind, nourish the spirit, and challenge the conscience. The publishing arm of the Maryknoll Fathers and Brothers, Orbis seeks to explore the global dimensions of the Christian faith and mission, to invite dialogue with diverse cultures and religious traditions, and to serve the cause of reconciliation and peace. The books published reflect the views of their authors and do not represent the official position of the Maryknoll Society. To learn more about Maryknoll and Orbis Books, please visit our website at www.orbisbooks.com.

Published by Orbis Books, Box 302, Maryknoll, NY 10545-0302.

Manufactured in the United States of America

Library of Congress Cataloging-in-Publication Data

Names: Brown, Brian, 1948- author.
Title: Earth's journey into hope : reflections on Thomas Berry's great work / Brian Edward Brown.
Description: Maryknoll, NY : Orbis Books, [2024] | Series: Ecology & justice series | Includes bibliographical references. | Summary: "A collection of spiritual reflections on the ecological theology of Thomas Berry"—Provided by publisher.
Identifiers: LCCN 2024007755 (print) | LCCN 2024007756 (ebook) | ISBN 9781626985797 (trade paperback) | ISBN 9798888660348 (epub)
Subjects: LCSH: Ecology—Religious aspects. | Nature—Religious aspects. | Berry, Thomas, 1914-2009.
Classification: LCC BT695.5 .B754 2024 (print) | LCC BT695.5 (ebook) | DDC 261.8/8—dc23/eng/20240429
LC record available at https://lccn.loc.gov/2024007755
LC ebook record available at https://lccn.loc.gov/2024007756

Contents

Prologue by Mary Evelyn Tucker   vii

A Note regarding Citation   xiii

Introduction   xv

1. Reflections on "The Great Work"   1

2. Reflections on "The Meadow across the Creek"   6

3. Reflections on "The Earth Story"   11

4. Reflections on "The North American Continent"   17

5. Reflections on "The Wild and the Sacred"   24

6. Reflections on "The Viable Human"   30

7. Reflections on "The University"   37

8. Reflections on "Ecological Geography"   43

9. Reflections on "Ethics and Ecology"   50

Contents

10. Reflections on "The New Political Alignment"   56

11. Reflections on "The Corporation Story"   62

12. Reflections on "The Extractive Economy"   69

13. Reflections on "The Petroleum Interval"   75

14. Reflections on "Reinventing the Human"   82

15. Reflections on "The Dynamics of the Future"   90

16. Reflections on "The Fourfold Wisdom"   99

17. Reflections on "Moments of Grace"   106

Epilogue: Cosmology and Ecology: Shaping the Earth Community by John Grim   113

References   117

Prologue

This collection of reflections on Thomas Berry's classic book, *The Great Work*, is one of the most probing illuminations of Berry's thought available. Berry's penetrating insights are lifted up for the reader to consider from many angles. Like a prism where the light shines through, Brian Brown offers perspectives like no other. As a doctoral student at Fordham, he absorbed Berry's intellectual breadth and spiritual depth in a unique manner. This included not only taking his classes for years but also living with him at the Riverdale Center of Religious Research while writing his doctoral thesis.

Brown illustrates Berry's foresight regarding our environmental and social challenges some twenty-five years ago when *The Great Work* was first published. The continued relevance of Thomas's ideas to our present circumstances is evident in Brian's remarkable commentary.

Prologue

As this book makes clear, we are living in a historical period that is requiring of us a monumental shift of consciousness and conscience. This is a time of immense ecological devastation, with crushing social consequences and unknown effects on the future of life itself. We need few reminders of what interrelated problems we are facing, such as climate change and climate refugees, species extinction and ecosystem loss, widespread pollution of land, air, and water with attendant health consequences.

In the midst of these polycrises, we draw strength from Thomas's responses to these challenges as described here by Brian. He highlights Berry's description of the "extractive economy" and the "petroleum interval" as well as the "new political alignment." He unpacks Berry's vision of the "viable human," which involves "reinventing the human." He comments on Berry's invitation to all the major institutions—politics, economics, education, and religion—to become involved in solutions to these problems.

We draw courage as well from the journey of Thomas himself as he uncovers the Great Work of our time. Growing up in the South, Thomas absorbed the rhythms of nature's beauty before development swept away "the meadow across the creek." Then heading north, he found his way to Western theology in the seminary when he entered the Passionist order of monks. Later he explored Western history and Native American traditions at Catholic University in Washington, DC, for his PhD. Moving beyond the West, he journeyed to China, where he encountered the religious traditions of Asia, especially Confucianism. He crossed over to Europe as an army chaplain after World War II. Returning to the United States, he found his way into teaching—at Seton Hall, at St. John's University, and finally at Fordham. Each one of these turns in Thomas's journey presented new challenges as he sought to discover the Great Work of our time.

- His professors at Catholic University did not understand the breadth of his interests and insisted that he pare down and rewrite his doctoral thesis.
- His time in China was cut short by Mao's army moving into Beijing in 1948, and he had to flee the country.
- His desire to teach was not initially affirmed by his religious order, as the Passionists are a monastic retreat community, not a teaching order.
- The robust History of Religions program that he created at Fordham was the section most attended by students, but it was not fully embraced by the theology department. Indeed, it was disassembled after Berry retired in 1979.
- The Riverdale Center of Religious Research that he founded in 1970 was discontinued, and the four-hundred-year-old great red oak behind it was cut down after he returned home to North Carolina in 1995.

Yet, amidst these obstacles and setbacks, Thomas never succumbed to bitterness or cynicism. Rather, he embraced his life journey with humor, in the company of friends, enriched by food and music on the sun porch at the Riverdale Center. For a quarter of a century, he nurtured us there, along the banks of the Hudson River, across from the 200-million-year-old cliffs of the Palisades, where we would gather with him to take in the luminous sunset.

Through our graduate studies and early teaching, there was Thomas, ready to go to the Broadway dinner, opening the Center for our monthly Teilhard lectures, moving through his immense library with his generous spirit: "Take this book; you will need it" was his mantra. How poignant it was when this mantra became the work of his eightieth year, as together we dismantled this splendid library of some ten thousand books, sending them like a shamanic dismemberment to scholars all over North America.

How can one capture the immense journey of such a person who always had time for each visitor—who made us all feel like his companions on the way?

This was a man of the great Dao—the Way beyond name or form, as the Daoists would say. He was a sage in the Confucian sense—forming one body with the Universe, the Earth, and the Ten Thousand Things. He was the Cosmic Person, the Mahapurusha of the Vedic Hymns of early Hinduism. He was, as he often explored in his writing, an *uomo universale,* namely, a person who was constantly broadening his vision.

It is the spirit of such a Cosmic Person that Brian Brown captures in his reflections. He sees with remarkable insight what Berry was articulating and gives us back a fresh view of the Great Work. Berry's analysis of the problems is as relevant as when it was first published, and his prescience is noteworthy. But Berry knew that analysis alone would not lead to transformation and engagement.

He realized we needed a vision to which we could dedicate our life—that is, a vision of the living Earth community in which we dwell and have our being. This calls us back to a wisdom path that we have lost—one in which the sentience of the world is speaking to us and evoking a response. This is Berry's genius—the poetic skill to awaken in us the lost mind and heart of the universe. This is Brown's attunement in seeing the Great Work as a calling—an invitation to participate in the symphony of life that surrounds us even now. The unraveling of life systems may be halted; a revived human species can be reimagined. Berry's Great Work is beckoning—not in the distance, but now, as future generations of all species listen and wait expectantly.

Mary Evelyn Tucker
Yale Forum on Religion and Ecology

A Note Regarding Citation

Throughout this book, citations and references to Thomas Berry's *The Great Work* appear as simple parenthetical citations with only the page number or page range. Where appropriate, citations to material other than *The Great Work* have fuller citations in parenthetical author-date citations.

The edition of *The Great Work* cited is Thomas Berry, *The Great Work: Our Way into the Future* (New York: Harmony/Bell Tower, 1999).

Introduction

In early September 1970, I took a seat in one of Dealy Hall's multiple classrooms on the Rose Hill campus of Fordham University in the Bronx, New York. Although beginning my senior year, I was still undecided about the future. As a double major in both theology and psychology, I was inclined to pursue graduate studies in clinical psychology and had begun to explore programs in that field. But ruminations about that possibility ceded their place just then to my customary anticipation about the course whose professor I was awaiting. The entirety of my theology classes until then had engaged me in some aspect of the Jewish and Christian traditions, so I was eager to explore "The Religions of China," about whose texts and teachings I had no studied acquaintance. Beyond the briefest description in the course catalog, I knew only that the professor was not one of Fordham's

Jesuits but was rather a Passionist priest by the name of Thomas Berry.

As autumn deepened, so did my appreciation for this remarkable voice who guided us with such clarity through the wisdom of the Confucian, Taoist, and Neo-Confucian traditions. In him, the illustrious teachings of Confucius, Mencius, Lao Tzu, Chuang Tzu, Chu Hsi, and Wang Yang-Ming all became articulate. My ambiguities about graduate study receded as that graced semester drew to its close. Through his fidelity and dedication to the Chinese ideal of the sage, the teacher-scholar, Thomas Berry had immeasurably expanded the spiritual and intellectual horizon toward which he gestured and I so distinctly now sought to follow.

Since he himself had founded the History of Religions doctoral degree program in Fordham's School of Theology, I was delighted to receive a full scholarship and serve as his teaching assistant during my years of graduate study under his guidance. In that capacity, I was able to observe his ever-gracious demeanor; ever available, ever encouraging, and supportive of all those enrolled in his courses, with particular attention to those concentrating in the expansive field of the History of Religions. While never failing in his personal warmth and pastoral sensibilities for each of his many graduate students, Thomas Berry schooled and held us to the highest standards of academic excellence, insisting on fidelity to primary texts and mastery of the broad cultural history and respective traditions from within which such texts arose and played their role. A measure of the breadth and depth of his own understanding of global religious history might be reflected in the fact that, until 1970, he was the sole faculty member teaching undergraduate and graduate classes in the Hindu, Buddhist, Confucian, and Taoist traditions, as well as the religions of the Indigenous peoples of North America. Even when relieved of teaching classes on Hinduism, through the additional faculty hire, he remained deeply engaged in its exposition by serving as the dissertation mentor and reader for those students who had done most of their doctoral coursework in that tradition under his initial guidance.

Thomas Berry had played a critical determinative role in orienting and broadening my appreciation and interest in religions beyond my native Catholicism during that initial graced moment of encounter in my senior year of undergraduate study. Over the years of graduate course work that followed, his influence remained constant, even if it was less dramatic.

My interest in interreligious dialogue was ever guided by his implicit insistence on attentive listening to the particular religious tradition being addressed through exacting, if not exhaustive, familiarity with the representative texts of that respective tradition.

To attempt otherwise was to subvert genuine mutual understanding at the deepest level and to trivialize the whole interreligious exercise in its most creative potential for further mutual interest and exploration.

He was ever the sage, teaching by his own example; his fidelity to texts as fundamental to respectful and authentic dialogue was exemplified in an account given by the eminent Chinese scholar William Theodore de Bary of Columbia University, who invited Thomas Berry to participate in the university's prestigious Seminar on Oriental Thought and Religion. At one such gathering, Berry presented a paper on the Shingon tradition, the most complex and esoteric school of Japanese Buddhism. Among the scholarly audience sat Yoshito Hakeda, one of the foremost translators of Buddhist texts on Columbia's faculty and who himself had studied to be a monk within the Shingon sect. At the close of Berry's reflection, de Bary noticed tears running quite visibly down Hakeda's cheeks. Upon inquiry, Hakeda explained that, as he listened to Berry, he thought that he heard the voice of his old master back in Japan. This account, which I heard directly from de Bary early in my graduate career and again much later in his eulogy at the memorial service at St. John the Divine shortly after Thomas Berry's death, remains iconic for Berry's capacity to reach deeply into the heart of another religious tradition. It also represents the rubric of that exacting attention and respectful familiarity with the voice of the other by precise familiarity with their texts.

The choice of texts to study when addressing another tradition is a matter of considered judgment, depending on the particular concept being explored, the metaphysical and psychological framework within which the concept finds meaningful expression, and the beliefs and practices through which the concept shapes and cultivates concrete human behavior. In the History of Religions, these broad considerations, among others, figure prominently in the choice one makes to pursue a particular idea as one's doctoral thesis. Of necessity, the very formulation of one's topic involves extensive and lengthy research before any writing even begins. Many professors who serve as dissertation mentors insist on meeting at set regular times for updates on the progress they expect from their doctoral candidates. Such was not my experience with Thomas Berry.

Having identified my initial interest in studying the concept of the Buddha Nature as the innate potentiality of all sentient beings to attain the supreme and perfect state of Enlightenment, I spoke to him about an initial text that had served as the basis of one of my doctoral comprehensive exam questions. When pressed what would be next, I admitted that I was not yet clear about that but would be in touch as my reading progressed. He agreed, with his customary warmth, and we parted, he in the doorway of his Riverdale Center for Religious Research on the Hudson River, as I returned to pressing family matters in Brooklyn.

After sending off my younger siblings to school each morning, I would read extensively until their return. Then again after dinner, I would read further into the early next morning. Some months passed before I found a second source text for my thesis. Back to Riverdale I went and explained the importance of the newly found sutra. As ever, after some questions, my mentor approved, and we said our goodbyes.

It would be over a year and a half before I had identified the five seminal texts and their supportive commentarial treatises needed to present a cogent interpretation of the metaphysical, epistemological, and soteriological dimensions of the Buddha Nature. Over the whole of that time, I would see Thomas Berry at occasional gatherings. These were often ones in which fellow graduate students, together with members of the American Teilhard Association, would congenially mingle after Thomas Berry, longtime president of the association, would present a penetrating reflection on some topic related to the famed Jesuit's prolific writings.

These wine, cheese, and potluck salons held at the Riverdale Center were filled with Berry's mirthful laughter, and he would never make even the slightest, however discrete, reference to the status of my research. He simply waited for me to bring forth whatever respective text my reading would next discover and present its cogency to the slowly emerging thesis. He never asked to see notes or provide written summaries of the texts I presented. He only made some brief inquiry or general observation and would encourage my continued reading.

It was an utter grace from Thomas Berry that I was able to pursue my interests at my own pace in that initial extensive period, formulating a coherent thesis and discovering the sources upon which my explication would rest. Without imposing artificial time constraints or requisite written drafts of chapters in progress, he implicitly vested me with the trust to keep listening intently to the texts whose wisdom would reveal the full contours of the concept I sought to understand more completely. So heartened was I by his confidence in my fidelity to the texts that, when the actual process of writing came, I asked that we might continue in the same pattern: I would show him the dissertation when I was done. When he inquired if I meant that I would show him each individual chapter as I finished it, I clarified that I intended not to show him any writing until the entirety of the thesis was complete. And so it was that, with his ever-generous and gracious agreement, Thomas Berry returned me to my familial Brooklyn horarium to begin the slow

pace of composing my study on Buddhist enlightenment, woven of sutras, sastras, and my commentary
upon them.

   After two years, with my youngest sibling hap-
pily settled into college but with four chapters of my
thesis still to be completed, I found myself drawn to
the possibility of continuing my project at the Riverdale Center for Religious Research, where Berry
lived at the time with John Grim, another doctoral
candidate in Fordham's History of Religions program. They were joined by Valerio Ortolani, a Jesuit
from Mexico also engaged in doctoral degree studies. When I spoke to him about the possibility of a
year's residency at the Center, with its inspiring vista
of river and Palisades as a welcome change from the
confines of the shadowy darkness of my alley-facing
bedroom, he wryly asked if he would be permitted to
see more of my writing if I were living under his roof.
I politely demurred that it was an integral piece and
that I was fully expectant of his criticism and edito-
rial demands when there was a finished manuscript
for his consideration. With that, he gave one of his
characteristically engaging laughs and asked when I
was ready to move into the second-floor room that he
had waiting for me.

   So began what Thomas Berry would regularly
describe as his "golden year," an enchanted time in
which we would spontaneously come together for

daily lunches and dinners, whose simple fare and for whose casual preparation John and I shared responsibility, while Berry assisted in the washing of pots, bowls, and plates. These meals were relaxed affairs in which Berry might share the core idea of a certain paper he was preparing to deliver, or report back on a conference where he might have offered the keynote address. John might discuss an aspect of his dissertation as it neared its completion, or his experience honing his nascent craft of teaching at a nearby college. For my part, I was content to sit, absorbing wisdom's light, like one of the many potted plants in the sunroom porch with its worn dining table around which we gathered. There was always laughter and the low background strains of a Beethoven trio or Schubert quintet, always the spontaneous quiet that eventually returned us to our respective pursuits of the afternoon or the darkened remains of the day.

I had come to the Riverdale Center to immerse myself more intensely in the Buddhist texts of my doctoral thesis, yet I was again the beneficiary of an immense intellectual horizon to which my esteemed teacher oriented my thought, much as he had in that initial graced encounter in my senior year of undergraduate study. Then, it was the rich heritage of Chinese thought that schooled my mind and heart. Now, a much vaster cosmic panorama summoned my attention.

Even as I sought fidelity to the art of sensitive listening and precise interpretation of the texts that figured prominently in my study of the Buddha Nature, Thomas Berry was attentively listening to the voices of Earth in the exigency of its waters, soils, atmosphere, and communities of flora and fauna. Here, he read the neglected text of the wayward human, lost in the fixation of its own technocratic conceit, oblivious to the immense harm it inflicted on the integral functioning of the planetary body. Even as I focused on the idiom of ancient Indian and Chinese Buddhist texts, my esteemed teacher was mastering the grammar of the universe story through his study of cosmology, astronomy, geology, chemistry, biology, and psychology. These would be the disciplines of Thomas Berry's study and reflection as I increasingly heard him tell the cosmic narrative, the great story, as we sat in that sunlit porch, under the branches of the great red oak just outside the door, with the tidal flow of the Hudson down the hill, and the glacial, tree-covered Palisades on the opposite shore.

Only the story of cosmogenesis, an astounding creativity unfolding over the immensity of time and extension in space, could restore the human from the morass of its present perdition. Moving in the integrity of its early particle structure, through its atomic, galactic, solar, and Earth emergence, the universe vested the human with the hopefulness of self-aware-

Introduction

ness, that we might recognize the lineage from which we arose and the nobility to which we are yet called in the great work of restoration and celebration of all to which we are related. Such is the gifted benefi-cence of Thomas Berry that, twenty-five years after their publication, his essays remain so instructive, his hopefulness still so vibrant.

1

Reflections on "The Great Work"

In the dire immediacy of the most intense domestic and international civil unrest, Thomas Berry directs our attention to the human past to orient us toward the global future. Earth's exigency can be all too easily dimmed by the preoccupation with those present matters of intrahuman crisis, but it is nevertheless paramount. Contemporary humanity will be defined in its species identity by our responsiveness to the preservation and healing of planetary integrity. We must turn from the commercial-industrial-extractive processes to which we remain heirs and participants. Such a task is what Berry calls our "Great Work," to which we are summoned by Earth in its grievous plight.

Beyond the physical devastation we have wreaked upon the planetary body, there remains the problematic birth of the human into a still-persistent mode of consciousness that is embodied in political, economic, intellectual, and religious establishments. This mentality embraces the conceit of consciousness as the sole purview of the human, derogating the status of other-than-human beings as exploitable objects devoid of any inherent value to which some notion of natural right would have afforded protection against human onslaught. Depriving rights of all but itself, the human has plundered Earth with impunity. But in its constriction of juridical recognition for itself alone, it has not only ravaged the planetary body but has excluded itself from that deepest sense of joy and fulfillment that arises from human continuity with, as Berry writes, the

> single integral community of the Earth that includes all its component members whether human or other than human. In this community every being has its own role to fulfill, its own dignity, its inner spontaneity. Every being has its own voice. Every being declares itself to the entire universe. Every being enters into communion with other beings. This capacity for relatedness, for presence to other beings, for spontaneity in action, is a capacity possessed by every mode of being throughout the entire universe. (4)

"The Great Work"

And so the pressing question, the definitive Great Work of the present, is the realignment of the human from its destructive self-aggrandizement and estranged alienation back into and within the dynamics of the cosmic-Earth process of its original emergence and integral identity. No past generation has had "the power to plunder Earth in its deepest foundations, with awesome impact on its geobiological structure, its chemical constitution, and its living forms throughout the wide expanse of the land and in the far reaches of the sea" (3). The singular destruction that humans have exacted has led to the enormity of the task now at hand.

The realignment of the human necessarily begins with the movement from the harms it has perpetrated even as it responds to the allure of the beauty and wonder of what remains of the living world. Within that renewed and centered position, the human is further disposed to draw indispensable psychic energy from its own past for the arduous movement into its future. Its own Great Work of planetary preservation and healing, as immense and distinct as it is, shares creative ancestry with earlier cultural achievements, earlier Great Works, from the multiple peoples and traditions that define its common species lineage. From across the wide range of their otherwise varied expressions and accomplishments, those forebears in the shared human venture may hearten and inspire contemporary descendants for the unique task we now assume.

Berry attends to a resistance that is proximate in culture and time to our own, those geographers, ethnologists, Indigenous elders, philosophers, landscape artists, land preservationists, and voices of the nineteenth century. Thoreau, Muir, Olmstead, the painters of the Hudson River School, the Audubon Society, Sierra Club, and Wilderness Society, and others sensed the despoliation of the American continent by the commercial-industrial juggernaut. They each and collectively lent their Great Works, giving voice to the sacrality of Earth, "a shrine," writes Berry, "that fulfill[s] some of the deepest emotional, imaginative and intellectual needs of the human soul" (6).

Critical strength and psychic resolve for the heaviness and uncertainty of what, now, must be borne come from further back in time and across cultures. The lustrous achievements, for example, of twelfth- and thirteenth-century European art, architecture, literature, and theology flowered in their brilliance in response to the violence and cultural decline of the six preceding centuries. Similarly, China's luminous expressions of Buddhist and Neo-Confucian thought of the T'ang and Sung dynasties followed upon the upheavals and disarray at the close of the earlier Han period. "We need to recall," writes Berry, "that in these and in so many other instances the dark periods of history are the creative periods, for these are the times when new ideas, arts, and institutions can be brought into being at the most basic level" (9).

Berry offers a perspective through which the looming shadows cast by the magnitude of the terminal phase of the Cenozoic era are even now illumined to reveal the indistinct contours of the dawning Ecozoic. The work that has begun, the work to which we are each and together called, the work of reinventing and inhabiting the political, economic, intellectual, and religious expressions for the preservation, healing, and celebration of the integral Earth community—that work draws its greatness not alone from the possibilities and accomplishments of the human past but from the very dynamics of universe creativity whence come our primordial emergence, abiding wisdom, and deepest fulfillment.

2

Reflections on "The Meadow across the Creek"

In the Maytime moment of meadow and creek, with its indelible impress on the boyhood sensibility of Thomas Berry, one discerns the breadth and depth of what would progressively unfold and become clarified over the years of his most mature thought and expression. The loveliness of lilies rose up from the meadow grasses to greet him together with the crickets, birdsong, distant woodlands, and passing clouds. Indeed, the immense creativity of the whole Earth revealed itself in the differentiated bioregional specificity of North Carolina soils, waters, springtime breezes, and all manner of fauna and flora inhabiting those domains.

This little patch of meadowland has none of
the majesty of the Appalachian or the western mountains, none of the immensity or the
power of the oceans, not even the harsh magnificence of desert country. Yet in this little
meadow the magnificence of life as celebration
manifested in a manner as profound and as
impressive as any other place I have known in
these past many years. (13–14)

Berry's meadow and creek are more than just some
isolated locale or mere site for exclusive and privileged
rumination. They are iconic of the extraordinary integration of the planetary body across the expanse of its
water and land mass, expressing its vibrancy in the
distinctive array of living beings that have blossomed
and flourished from within its dynamic sequence of
transformations. Earth's body, as meadow and creek,
addressed Berry with a critical and salient dimension
that left a lasting and determinative imprint on the
whole of his life's orientation and body of thought.

For almost the entirety of our ancestral past,
humans have been a deeply celebratory species, evi-
denced in the rich panoply of ritual and ceremonial
expressions over the range of our collective habitation throughout the planet. Humans have always
responded to the variegated constellation of those
waters, soils, fauna, and flora of the respective bio-

region wherein ritual and ceremony were enacted. Celebrations in word and gesture have embedded human consciousness in the body of Earth from which it has emerged and by which it is sustained.

> From Paleolithic times humans have coordinated their ritual celebrations with the transformation moments of the natural world. Ultimately, the universe, throughout its vast extent in space and its sequence of transformations in time, was seen as a single, multiform celebratory expression. No other explanation seems possible for the world that we see around us. The birds fly and sing; they build their nests and raise their young. The flowers blossom. The rains nourish every living being. The tides flow back and forth. The seasons succeed each other in an entrancing sequence. Each of the events in the natural world is a poem, a painting, a drama, a celebration. (18)

Over uncounted millennia and in the still-vibrant resiliency of contemporary Indigenous traditions, humans have chanted and danced our solidarity, our communion, with all the other-than-human beings in the liturgy of Earth.

It is now necessary to retrieve and renew this innate human disposition from the calamity of the industrial-commercial phase of the last several centuries. Absent all trace of celebration but for its own technical mastery and triumph over the natural world, this phase has rendered the Earth body a wasteland of fungible, commodified resources. Yet as the destructiveness of that reductively materialistic, mechanistic, and mercantile mentality has reached ascendancy, its sterility has exposed the deep human longing for intimacy and fulfillment with meadow and creek, crickets and songbirds, lilies and grasses.

> The proposal has been made that no effective restoration of a viable mode of human presence on the planet will take place until such intimate human rapport with the Earth community and the entire functioning of the universe is reestablished on an extensive scale. Until this is done the alienation of the human will continue despite the heroic efforts being made towards a more benign mode of human activity in relation to Earth. The present is not a time of desperation but for hopeful activity. (19)

Beyond cultivating within ourselves that communion capacity with Earth in the immediacy of wherever it reveals itself to us, two endeavors of Berry's "hopeful activity" may lie in an attentiveness to the mind of the child on the one hand and the liturgical creativity of religious traditions on the other. To compensate for the alienation and harm of generations of illiteracy in reading the book of nature, a primary concern in the education of children must be to situate them within the unfolding story of the universe, to activate that innate sense of wonder and delight in their kinship and care for all beings of the living Earth as common home. A hopeful future may likewise emerge among those religious communities who, across otherwise different beliefs, may consolidate themselves around that same sacred story and discover new wisdom and spiritual vitality in the celebratory expressions and protective ethos that story may yet evoke.

> The work before us is the task not simply of ourselves but of the entire planet and all its component members. While the damage that has been done is immediately the work of humans, the healing cannot be the work simply of humans any more than the illness of one organ of the body can be healed through the efforts of that one organ. Every member of the body must bring about the healing. So now the entire universe is involved in the healing of the damaged Earth in the light and warmth of the sun. (20)

3

Reflections on "The Earth Story"

If the modern human is to avert our own demise and cease our marauding mentality toward Earth, we are in dire need of tremendous psychic energy both to disengage from our destructiveness and to address our profound alienation from the planetary body. To recover the lost identity of the latter is to remediate the harm of the former. Where again will the modern human discover the deep reserve of psychic energy for such a venture to realize its intrinsic rootedness within Earth? Where again will we experience the depths of energy so as to activate and galvanize the array of pressing, practical measures to heal, preserve, and enhance planetary integrity and viability into the future?

For Thomas Berry, the requisite creativity for the present and future cannot be secured merely by appropriating or replicating an Earth–human continuity from cultural experience and celebrations arising from the past. Undoubtedly, though, a depth of wisdom and beauty that may resonate powerfully in contemporary minds and hearts from the broad heritage of human intimacy with the larger cosmic reality may remain.

Neo-Confucian China offers the consistent ideal of the human as the understanding heart of Heaven and Earth, forming one body with them and the myriad beings inhabiting them. Even now, across cultures and centuries, there arises a compelling evocative response from the opening lines of Chang Tsai's eleventh-century *Western Inscription*:

> Heaven is my father and Earth is my mother, and even such a small creature as I finds an intimate place in their midst. Therefore, that which fills the universe I regard as my body and that which directs the universe I consider as my nature. All people are my brothers and sisters, and all things are my companions. (Chan 1969, 497)

A similar orientation of the human within the more encompassing communion of animate Earth is as instructive as it is distinct. The seven principal rituals of the Lakota culture of the North American plains formally acknowledge, respectfully invoke, and consistently refer to the whole community of life as one's kin, one's relatives, who are intrinsic participants with their respective wisdom and power in every ceremonial experience. Absent the whole community of life's indispensable presence, ritual is so much sterile human gesture, devoid of depth and transformative vitality. This sense of an integral cosmic plenitude where all beings are mutually present to one another and together celebrate the numinous reality whence all have come finds expression in the symbolism of the sweat lodge.

> The willows which make the frame of the sweat lodge are set up in such a way that they mark the four quarters of the universe; thus, the whole lodge is the universe in an image, and the two-legged, four-legged and winged peoples, and all things of the world are contained within it, for all these peoples and things too must be purified before they can send a voice to Wakan Tanka [the Great Spirit]. (Black Elk and Brown 1953, 32)

Intrinsic to all Lakota liturgy, the sweat lodge is the space for initial prayer before any further ritual expression might be engaged. As such, its simple circular form, made of willow tree branches and covered by buffalo hide, both belies and denotes its profound significance.

Such examples, and so many others, identify the human capacity to recognize and celebrate a more comprehensive, expansive, and numinous Earth community. Yet, even as they retain a certain potency to instruct and inspire, those earlier traditions and their stories arose within modes of human consciousness that were incapable of explicitly addressing the reality of the present crisis.

> We cannot do without our earlier experiences of the numinous presence manifested in the great Cosmic Liturgy. We cannot do without our humanistic traditions, our art and poetry and literature. But these traditions cannot themselves simply with their own powers, do what needs to be done. These earlier experiences and accomplishments were dealing with other issues, providing guidance for different worlds than the world of the early twenty-first century. To meet the current environmental challenge they too need to be transformed within the context of an emergent universe. (24–25)

These experiences and traditions arose in a mode of consciousness unformed by an understanding of the cosmos as a processive, dynamic development that thoroughly imbeds the human within it and for which the human bears intrinsic responsibility for its extension and flourishing into the future.

"The Earth Story"

We no longer live simply in a spatial mode of consciousness where time is experienced as a seasonal renewing sequence of realities that keep their basic identity in accord with the Platonic archetypal world. We now live not so much in a *cosmos* as in a *cosmogenesis*; that is, a universe ever coming into being through an irreversible sequence of transformations moving in the larger arc of its development from a lesser to a great[er] order of complexity and from a lesser to a great[er] consciousness. (26)

The integrity and coherence of the cosmogenetic process dispose contemporary humans to that plenitude of psychic energy so critical to extricating ourselves from the narrow confines of our technocratic self-absorptions, including the dangerous impasse through which our industrial-commercial fixation threatens Earth and, of necessity, ourselves. "The human," writes Berry, "is neither an addendum nor an intrusion into the universe. We are quintessentially integral with the universe. In ourselves the universe is revealed to itself as we are revealed in the universe" (32). By delineating the comprehensive, holistic trajectory of an immense creativity unfolding over some 13.8 billion years of universe becoming, and by identifying the emergence of the human within that process, cosmogenesis restores the human to our true stature and role not as alien and extrinsic

15

master but as intrinsic participant within universe creativity itself.

Tracing our cosmic lineage to its deepest roots, and through the exactitude of observational science, the human recognizes our point of origin in the flaring forth of stupendous primordial energy that soon began to shape and consolidate itself into the sub-atomic particle structures that subsequently coalesced as hydrogen and helium and whose gravitational compression combusted in the incandescence of the hundreds of billions of galaxies. Then, in the local Milky Way, cosmogenesis further advanced its creativity through the thermodynamics of supernova collapse, manifesting the novelty of chemical elements that, in turn, shaped the Sun and its eight orbiting planets.

Only Earth, elegant in size and distance from its star, would yield a lithosphere, hydrosphere, and atmosphere, blossoming into a biosphere. From within its Cenozoic flourishing, cosmogenesis-as-human recognizes, reflects upon, and celebrates the wonder and mystery of its Source and of ourselves in the integrity and impeccable intimacy of Earth's differentiated manifestations throughout vast extensions in space and transformations in time. Instructive and therapeutic, this is the telling from the deepest past that clarifies our gaze and orients our hopeful engagement for the rigors and promise of the future.

4

Reflections on *"The North American Continent"*

In his essay on the North American continent, Thomas Berry continues to reflect on the dynamic creativity of the universe as it reached a critical, indeed dangerous, moment in its billionfold-long self-emergence. The drama arose and still seeks resolution in two quite distinctive modes of consciousness within the human sphere of universe expression: that of the First Peoples, who became indigenous to the continent on the one hand, and that of the much later European colonizers on the other.

Beginning some sixteen thousand years ago, the First Peoples, migrating from Asia across the Bering Strait, moved into the vast expanse of the North

American continent's land and water mass. These diverse peoples settled into the mountain ranges, prairies and grasslands, rivers and valleys, coastal shores and their adjacent plains, eastern forests, southern swamplands, western deserts, and deep canyons. While the first two millennia of their presence had a severe impact on continental fauna, their succeeding generations conformed and adapted to a more sustainable living within the biological constraints imposed by the regional climate variations and the respective communities of plants and animals abiding therein.

Over time, their intimacy with those other-than-human beings among whom they dwelt became a notable feature of First Peoples sensibility and consciousness. The Native peoples were highly differentiated across the range of geographic locales, speaking hundreds of languages, and developing and observing countless cultural traditions and lifeways. Amid this diversity, they nevertheless shared an attentiveness to the continent's communion of subjects, whose wisdom and guidance gave zest and resilience for the rigors of life's journey.

One of the most impressive examples of such an orientation, such a mode of consciousness, may be found in the ceremony of the Omaha people upon presenting a newborn to the cosmic community. In this way a child might be blessed in traversing the

four hills of childhood, youth, adulthood, old age,
and final return to the First Spirit:

O you sun, moon and stars
All of you that move in the heavens,
I bid you hear me,
Into your midst has come a new life.
Consent, I implore, make its path smooth
That it may reach the brow of the first hill.
O ye winds, clouds, rains, mist,
All of you that move in the air,
I bid you hear me,
Into your midst has come a new life.
Consent, I implore, make its path smooth
That it may reach the brow of the second hill.
O ye winds, valleys, rivers, lakes, trees, grasses,
All of you that belong to the earth, I bid you
    hear me.
Into your midst has come a new life.
Consent, I implore, make its path smooth
That it may reach the brow of the third hill.
Birds, great and small, that fly in the air;
Animals, great and small, that dwell in the for-
    est;
Insects that creep among the grasses and bur-
    row in the ground;
I bid you hear me,
Into your midst has come a new life.

Consent, I implore, make its path smooth
That it may reach the brow of the fourth hill.
All of you in the heavens, all of you in the
    waters, all of you in the earth, I bid you—
    all of you—to hear me.
Into your midst has come a new life.
Consent, consent,
All of you consent, I implore,
Make its path smooth that it may travel beyond
    the fourth hill.

                (Olson and Miller [Thio-um-Baska]
                            1979, 5–6)

Not only at birth but consistently over the course
of a lifetime through the richly variegated ceremoni-
alism of Native liturgies, human consciousness integrated and embedded itself within that encompassing
community of subjects. In addition to more explicitly
communal rituals, there were those like the Lakota
"Crying for a Vision" that afforded individual tribal
members, through solitary mountaintop prayer, to
intensify their relationship with all one's other-than-
human relatives. Black Elk, the Oglala holy man,
explained:

All these people are important, for in their
own way they are wise and they can teach
us two-leggeds much if we make ourselves
humble before them. . . . This will help you to

understand in part how it is that we regard all created beings as sacred and important, for everything has a *"wochangi"* or influence which can be given to us, through which we may gain a little more understanding if we are attentive. (Black Elk and Brown 1953, 58–59)

This profound receptivity to be tutored and enriched in intimacy with the numinous dimensions of the North American continent's communion of subjects found no resonance in the colonizing mentality that overwhelmed its shores with the European onslaught.

In stark contrast to the cosmo-biocentric orientation of Native consciousness, the European mindset was fatally closed in upon, and captivated by, its own extreme anthropocentrism. The European mind was formed by the influence of the Greek humanist tradition, the primacy of the divine–human relationship in the Christian tradition, the subordination of land to mere property with the human as sole bearer of rights in its legal tradition, and the maximization of profit through commercial-industrial exploitation of resources in its ascendant mercantile tradition. Combined, all four cultural conceits defined a European mode of consciousness in the isolation of its own inflated self-absorptions with minimal regard for any inherent value in the commodified world of its conquest. Berry describes the European mindset, writing:

As seen by the Europeans the continent was here to serve human purposes through trade and commerce as well as through the more immediate personal and household needs of the colonists. They had nothing spiritual to learn from this continent. . . . The insuperable difficulty inhibiting any intimate rapport with the continent or its people was this European-derived anthropocentrism. . . . That is why the North American continent became completely vulnerable to the assault from the European peoples. To the European settlers the continent had no sacred dimension. It had no inherent rights. It had no way of escaping economic exploitation. The other component members of the continent could not be included with humans in an integral continental community. European presence was less occupation than predation. (44–45)

We now live in the aftermath of this encounter. We are several centuries into continental-become-planetary ruination. Ours is the challenge to initiate concrete, practical choices and policies for the protection, preservation, and healing of what remains. The determination and effort required will be immense, for the venture involves nothing less than the reinvention of the human at the globalized species level.

"The North American Continent"

We dare not assume the daunting task before us by our own devices alone. We turn in hope to the cosmic community that yet extends itself for the rebirth now upon us. And so, we invoke:

> All of you in the heavens, all of you in the waters,
> All of you in the earth,
> We bid you—all of you—to hear us.
> Into your midst has come a new life.
> Consent, consent,
> All of you consent, we implore,
> Make its path smooth
> That it may ascend this most arduous and steepest hill.

5

Reflections on "The Wild and the Sacred"

The commercial-industrial human submitted to scant self-restraint even as it extended itself throughout the planetary body, advancing its technocratic subjugation and consumptive exploitation of Earth's soils, waters, atmosphere, and diverse biota of every kind inhabiting those realms. The human, seeking to harness and tame the natural world as alien and distinct from itself, the mastery mentality of technocratic consciousness, in failing to bridle its own impulses, has rendered Earth desolate.

We misconceive our role if we consider that our historical mission is to "civilize" or to "domesticate" the planet, as though wildness is something destructive rather than the ultimate creative modality of any form of earthly being. We are not here to control. We are here to become integral with the larger Earth community. The community itself and each of its members has ultimately a wild component, a creative spontaneity that is its deepest reality, its most profound mystery. . . . I bring all this to mind because we are discovering our human role in a different order of magnitude. We are experiencing a disintegration of the life systems of the planet just when the Earth in the diversity and resplendence of its self-expression had attained a unique grandeur. . . . In our efforts to reduce the planet to human control we are, in reality, terminating the Cenozoic Era, the lyric period of life development on the Earth. (48–49)

If, then, we are to move beyond the deadly debacle of domination to become integral with and as Earth we must fully appreciate that self-restraint, rather than diminishing human potential, is the very principle through which we become fully participant in cosmic creativity.

The universe emerged and continued to unfold in the exquisite balance between the wild, exuberant, expansive energy and the complementary discipline of containment and limitation. Without the primordial restraint of gravity, the originating flaring forth of stupendous cosmic radiance would have ended in mere dispersal, preventing the universe from consolidating itself into the particle, atomic, and galactic structures of its further self-manifestation. That ongoing creativity of universe emergence through the interplay of wild, expansive dispersion and restraining containment is likewise operative in the thermodynamics of supernova events, where the wild, explosive scattering of elements and gas released by the collapse of a dying star is retrieved and gathered by the discipline of gravity to eventually constellate, in our local region of the Milky Way some five billion years ago, a new star, our Sun, and its eight orbiting planets.

That same exquisite balance of cosmic creativity between an excess of wild turbulence and an excess of confining limitation next expressed itself in the singular shaping of Earth. The geophysical structure of Earth is unlike the massive, wild gaseousness of Jupiter or the smaller, delimiting, rocky solidity of Mars. In the dynamic interaction of its elementally rich inner core and outer surface, Earth's structure provided the stability for the yet-more-fluid interdependence of its soils, waters, and atmosphere to eventually blossom into living cells.

Over hundreds of millions of years, the universe-as-animate Earth would yield ever more complex organisms woven into ever more complex interdependencies.

As it had in its primordial emergence and throughout the eons of its unfoldment, the universe remained constant in the creative principle now manifesting in the biosphere of Earth. Each novel being to emerge within the global community of life embodied the wild exuberance of the cosmos within the specific spontaneities of its own expressive movements and functions—putting forth roots in soils; soaring and gliding on wings; crawling or racing on four feet or more; swimming in watery depths, or burrowing in dens.

But whatever the expansive vitality of shape, sound, color, and movement in the countless modalities of Earth's fauna and flora, there could be thriving only within the demands imposed by the specific limitations of the respective soils, waters, atmosphere, and other established inhabitants of the local bioregion where any new being might arise or migrate. There can be no flourishing of novel life-forms without attentive conformity to the constraints of the larger community. Wild innovation is consistently creative only in the complementarity of disciplined self-limitation. If that is true in the shaping and articulation of its primordial and large-scale structures, the universe insists on that in its self-expression as planetary biosphere. So it is that Thomas Berry writes:

> We mistake the wild if we think of it as mere random activity or simply as turbulence.

27

Throughout the entire world there exists a discipline that holds the energies of the universe in the creative pattern of their activities, although this discipline may not be immediately evident to human perception. The emergent universe appears as some wild, senseless deed that wells up from some infinite abyss in the expansive differentiating process of those first moments when all the energy that would ever exist flared forth in a radiation too mysterious for humans to fully comprehend. . . . We might consider, then, that the wild and the disciplined are the two constituent forces of the universe, the expansive force and the containing force bound into a single universe and expressed in every being in the universe. . . . The universe from the beginning, and even now is poised between expanding and containing forces. . . . In this mysterious balance the universe and all its grandeur and loveliness become possible. Exactly here the presence of the sacred reveals itself. (51–53)

The tragedy of the commercial-industrial technocratic human is its utter failure to recognize and be guided by the cosmological wisdom of self-restraint. Absent the discipline of prudent self-evaluation and consequential foresight, and in the blind assumption

that its ingenuity and inventiveness were unequivo-
cally progressive, the human unleashed a wildness
neither creative nor sacred. In its excess of self-infla-
tion and entranced by the magic of mechanism and
the fantasies of consumerist desire, it has laid waste
the body of Earth.

But if the future is one of deepest foreboding at the
gravity of the harm that has been inflicted, the contemporary human yet retains that innate spontaneity
of wisdom to recognize the untenable destructiveness of what has been wrought in the terminal phase
of the Cenozoic. That same wisdom has begun to suggest whole new modes of creative Ecozoic living. Even
now, the contours of that human reinvention clarify in
divestment from the fossil-fuel industry; fully decar-
bonized, renewable energy systems; green housing
and urban design; public, electrified, and bipedal
transportation; revised and renewed agricultural and
animal husbandry practices; soil and water conserva-
tion innovations; restoration of wetlands and massive
variegated reforestation; and Earth-informed economics, jurisprudence, and education. In all of these
endeavors, the cosmos yet moves within the human
to live for the primacy of planetary flourishing and,
while holding fast to the discipline of its own delimiting and derivative status, to nevertheless actualize a
depth of wild creativity for the unfoldment that still
beckons.

6

Reflections on "The Viable Human"

At a time of gravest peril to the integral flourishing of Earth through the persistence of the
commercial-industrial onslaught of the last several
centuries of corporate domination and exploitation
of the planetary body, the question of human viability cannot be summarily dismissed. Yet, even in the
somber recognition of its harmfulness in plain sight
among Earth's waters, soils, atmosphere, and disappearing fauna and flora, human destructiveness is
not conclusive.

The universe, in full continuity with its radiant
emergence 13.8 billion years ago, still stirs powerfully
in the depths of the collective human psyche. The
universe continues to elicit and galvanize that same

creativity with which it shaped the galaxies, solar system, and Earth to now correct, realign, and animate human consciousness to its fullness of cosmic identity. "The universe itself," Berry writes, "is *the* enduring reality and *the* enduring value even while it finds expression in a continuing sequence of transformations" (56). In and through the dynamism of the archetypal symbols of the Journey, the Cosmic Tree, the Great Mother, and Death–Rebirth, the universe expands human understanding beyond the narrow confines of its destructive self-absorptions and consumerist cravings to realize its profound participation in the still-unfolding creativity of the universe itself.

As Journey, the universe narrates its self-emergence from the particle, atomic, and galactic expressions on into its solar and planetary manifestations with singular vibrancy as Earth, from whose body it birthed the human with its nobility as that being in whom the universe attains a distinctive self-awareness. In the complementary symbol of the Cosmic Tree, the universe further impresses and ratifies itself within human consciousness as a single, indivisible, organic reality with roots in the most profound past and whose trunk and branches extend throughout the vast extensions of darkest matter and luminous galaxies to blossom in the fruitfulness of Earth from whose human expression the universe marvels and celebrates its cosmic plenitude and integral creativity. The maternal nature of that creativity attains all the more clarity and powerful consolidation in the collective human psyche through the application of the Great Mother archetypal symbol to the universe–Earth reality. In tandem with the Journey and the Cosmic Tree, the image of the Great Mother elicits within human consciousness a radically transformed self-understanding, a conception in which humanity is no longer the dominant master but becomes both offspring and progenitor of cosmic creativity.

> We might now recover our sense of the maternal aspect of the universe in the symbol of the Great Mother, especially in the Earth as that maternal principle out of which we are born and by which we are sustained. Once this symbol is recovered the dominion of the patriarchal principle that has brought such aggressive attitudes into our activities will be mitigated. If this is achieved then our relationship with the natural world would undergo one of its most radical readjustments since the origins of our civilization in classical antiquity. (69–70)

The universe powerfully activates toward the re-education of human consciousness beyond assumptions and conceits of an anthropo- and androcentric past and its commercial rapacity of the planetary body. The archetype of Death–Rebirth, then, steels and readies that newly awakened, cosmic-informed consciousness for the demanding challenges yet ahead. The movement toward a restored Earth, pre-served and protected from further ravages to its waters, soils, and atmosphere, is a function of the most intense discipline and restraint by the human against the habitual conditioning and impulses of its consumptive past. This restraint is accompanied by humanity's dedicated resolve to scrutinize the whole range of our civilizational processes in language, law, education, medicine, commerce, and religion.

> Any recovery of the natural world in its full splendor will require . . . a conversion expe-rience deep in the psychic structure of the human. Our present situation is the conse-quence of a cultural fixation, an addiction, an emotional insensitivity, none of which can be remedied by any quickly contrived adjust-ment. Nature has been severely, and in many cases irreversibly, damaged. A healing is often available and new life can sometimes be evoked, but this cannot be without an inten-sity of concern and sustained vigor of action such as that which brought about the damage in the first place. (60)

So then, a biocentric orientation and sensibility must necessarily reclaim, infuse, and expand the language of "progress" and "profit" from their centuries-long capture within a corporate culture that has skillfully manipulated these terms to exclude all cost to the planetary body as mere externalities to the respective commercial enterprise. With sophisticated and massive propaganda and an artificially contrived pricing scheme, corporate profit has been amassed and progress has been made for shareholders and a consuming public even as the natural world has been plundered and pervasively weakened. The present and ongoing challenge is to expose the irrational illusion of commercial profit and progress at the expense and to the deficit of Earth.

Biocentric reclamation will be immeasurably aided by corresponding developments within both medicine and law. Because it is axiomatic that human health is unsustainable on a toxic and degraded planet and that a healed Earth is the prescriptive condition for human well-being, it is all the more imperative that law extend its protection to the natural world and the other-than-human beings of its global community. If Earth has become vulnerable to the plunderous profiteering of the corporate commercial enterprise, if the health and integral resilience of its waters, soils, and atmosphere have become so critically debilitated and severely threatened, law's complicity must be confronted and reversed.

Reducing the natural world to mere property, with all notion of rights reserved solely to the human as proprietor and landlord, law has long consigned and condoned Earth's bondage as commodified resources and chattel whose ultimate disposition was at the discretion of those holding title or exercising possession. The ruination of such a legal scheme can no longer be defended. The weight of the injurious evidence is too preponderant to exclude or exculpate. If law is to retain its privileged position for stability and well-being within communities, it must now accord its full recognition and extend its protections for the values and contributions of each being in the immeasurably expanded community of integral Earth. No less effort will be needed in the re-valorization of education and religion as that in the renewal of language, commerce, health, and law. But if the task of conforming human cultural processes within the limitations of the planetary body is daunting, nothing less than the universe itself journeys, blossoms, and births within our endeavor.

> We must recognize that the only effective program available as our primary guide toward a viable human mode of being is the program offered by Earth itself. . . . Within this functional cosmology we can overcome our alienation and begin the renewal of life on a sustainable basis. This story is a numinous

revelatory story that could evoke not only the vision but also the energies needed for bringing ourselves and the entire planet into a new order of survival. (71)

7

Reflections on "The University"

As evidence of catastrophic climate collapse becomes increasingly ominous, human agency for planetary demise is irrefutable.

> So awesome is the devastation we are bringing about that we can only conclude that we are caught in a severe cultural disorientation, a disorientation that is sustained intellectually by the university, economically by the corporation, legally by the Constitution, spiritually by religious institutions. The universities might well consider their own involvement in our present difficulties. (73)

While all four domains of human cultural expression and their respective institutional establishments bear responsibility for the gravity that now menaces Earth, human insight and understanding, in its comprehensive regard and critical analysis as university, provides guidance not otherwise found in religion, economics, or law. In its commitment to the empirical observation of its sciences, the university is able to reveal Earth in the dynamism of its primordial formation and the geochemical and biological integrity of its evolutionary development. The university's disclosure of living Earth in its history and wholeness identifies its preeminence beyond religion's myopic scrutiny of written scriptures and commentaries, beyond law's parochial construal of constitutional texts arrogating all rights to the human and derogating Earth as mere property, beyond an economic prejudice for accounting ledgers that falsify profits by severely discounting and utterly ignoring cost to planetary waters, soils, atmosphere, and other living beings.

Beyond those cultural fixations and their failings, the university demonstrates the unitive cohesion and dynamic interdependence of Earth's lithosphere, hydrosphere, atmosphere, and biosphere as the context from within which the human emerged and whose reflective capacities began the elaboration of Earth as noosphere. It is, in fact, from within this global sphere of thought that the contemporary university confirms the integral continuity of the human with the whole of the Earth process that brought it into being and by which it is sustained.

> If the central pathology that has led to the termination of the Cenozoic is the radical discontinuity established between the human and the nonhuman, then the renewal of life on the planet must be based on the continuity between the human and the other than human as a single integral community. Once the continuity is recognized and accepted, then we will have fulfilled the basic condition that will enable the human to become present to the Earth in a mutually enhancing manner. (80)

But if the university recognizes the continuity of the human with and as an inherent dimension of Earth, it amplifies and deepens that coherence by extending its understanding of Earth into the unfolding dynamics of that cosmic immensity from which it was shaped. To understand the human is to understand Earth. To understand Earth is to understand the universe. To understand the universe is to peer back across some 13.8 billion years to that primordial flaring forth of astounding creativity, the quantum seed containing in itself all that would blossom as particles, atoms, galaxies, solar systems, planets, and, from within Earth, as microorganisms, mollusks, mayflies, magnolias, and mammals, that exuberant diversity of life among whom the universe would birth the human.

Thus it is that the universe reveals itself as story, that coherent sequence of emergence whose hearing immeasurably expands and clarifies the self-understanding of an alienated and prodigal human. In such a telling, consciousness, awareness, interiority, self-organization don't appear in isolation as the discrete and exclusive property of the human. They are found, rather, throughout the full range of universe self-expression from the particle and atomic structures through the full array of animate beings. To fully appreciate this profound continuity is to effect one of the most significant and crucial transformations of the human psyche with unparalleled consequence for the natural world of its present peril.

> We must consider that modes of consciousness exist throughout the universe in a vast number of qualitatively diverse manifestations. Above all we discover that every being has its own spontaneities that arise from the depths of its own being. These spontaneities express the inherent value of each being in such a manner that we must say of the universe that it is a communion of subjects, not a collection of objects. Precisely in this intimate relationship with the entire universe we overcome the

mental fixation of our times expressed in the radical division we make between the human and the other-than- human. This fixation that I have described as an unfeeling relation of the human to the natural world is healed in its deepest root as soon as we perceive that the entire universe is composed of subjects to be communed with, not primarily of objects to be exploited. (82)

With this animate and communal cosmology at its heart, the contemporary university weakens the sway of an earlier inexplicable natural terror, a philosophic arrogance, and a reductionistic nihilism that have long combined to effect a pernicious human estrangement from the natural world. The fearsome trauma of the fourteenth-century Black Death, the invidious dualism of seventeenth-century Cartesian mechanism, and a still-persistent scientific materialism have disaggregated all physical complexity to but the random happenstance of just so many directionless elemental structures. Against the comprehensive breadth, intellectual persuasiveness, and emotional invigoration of its living cosmology, the university exposes the unreasonable fears, untenable conceits, and profound disorientation worked by this threesome, which it so thoroughly discredits and authoritatively refutes.

Beyond that corrective, the university in its living cosmology yet works for the reclamation and reanimation of economics, religion, and law. Each of these three other fundamental expressions of human culture must, in their own discipline, attend to the universe telling its story in the full communion of its subjects as they principally manifest in the one body of Earth. Each must discover its own capacity to reinvent a human mode of living within that body that appreciates its inestimable and ever-renewing value, celebrates its inherent sanctity, and recognizes its inalienable right warranting its most zealous preservation and effective protection.

8

Reflections on "Ecological Geography"

At its heart, Thomas Berry's essay on "Ecological Geography" addresses intimacy with the comprehensive integral Earth community in and through its multiplicity of bioregional particularities. Such intimacy with the richly differentiated expressions of organic Earth is a summons to the collective human species for the most thorough self-examination and consequent self-restraint in the commercial-industrial-consumptive rapacity that has progressively debilitated and dangerously destabilized the planetary body. Significantly, a holistic integration of Earth in its bioregional specificities and the mounting clear and present danger from the collective human failure of self-restraint feature prominently in the Sixth

Assessment Report of the Intergovernmental Panel on Climate Change (IPCC), published in August of 2021. In its "Headline Statements from the Summary for Policymakers," the report notes soberly that

> It is unequivocal that human influence has warmed the atmosphere, ocean and land. . . . The scale of recent changes across the climate system . . . are unprecedented. . . . Human induced climate change is already affecting many weather and climate extremes in every region across the globe . . . heat waves, heavy precipitation, droughts and tropical cyclones and in particular their attribution to human influence has strengthened. . . . Global surface temperatures will continue to increase . . . during the 21st century unless deep reductions of carbon dioxide (CO_2) and other greenhouse gas emissions occur in the coming decades. (IPCC, "Headline Statements")

The IPCC Assessment Report and Thomas Berry share a conceptualization of a bioregionally integrated Earth severely threatened by human activity. The IPCC Assessment especially details the physical evidence of the harm. Importantly, Thomas Berry elucidates the psychic failure of human self-restraint as the root cause of that harm.

In the dynamic interaction of its lithosphere, hydrosphere, and atmosphere manifested as biosphere, Earth eventually blossomed in the profusion of its Cenozoic diversity. As it did so, Earth consistently ensured its cohesive self-integration across the ever more complex flora and fauna that it birthed through the wisdom and discipline of the niche. Each being, as it entered into the organic tapestry of Earth's weave, was genetically endowed with the ability to live within the possibilities afforded by the dynamic combination of water, soil, atmosphere, and the established plant and animal organisms of the respective bioregion where the newcomer emerged or into which it migrated. Each novel life-form, either through the spontaneity of mutation or arrival from elsewhere, would assume its role or flourish in its niche only in its conformity to the limitations and demands—that is, the possibilities—imposed by the larger community of its future sustenance and thriving. To ignore those conditions, through an ill-adaptive anatomy, excessive rates of nutrient consumption, or generation of progeny, would be to jeopardize an organism's fit within, and ultimate rejection by, the community of its nonconformance.

But if Earth continued its prolific creativity and self-coherence through the delicate balancing and finality of niche compatibility, it eventually fashioned a profoundly ambiguous, if not dangerous, innovation in the human species with its capacity to elude the otherwise protective limitations of niche constraint.

> In some sense the human refuses to accept any particular niche, for the basic function of a niche is to set limits to the activity of a species. In this sense the human refuses to accept limits imposed from without or even from within its own being. . . . Survival of any group of living beings in relation to other groups depends on the recognition of limits in the actions of each group. This law of limits is among the most basic of all cosmological, geological or biological laws. . . . Yet in the modern world this sense of limits imposed by the natural functioning of the universe has to some extent been overridden, at least in a temporary manner, by industrial processes created by humans. (91–92)

The calamitous impact of such heedless disregard for boundaries and living within their salutary confines is the dire chronicle of the IPCC's Sixth Assessment Report.

To understand this deadly impasse is to note that, among all its other living progeny, from the cellular to the more elaborate mammalian expressions, Earth endowed the human with the genetic wisdom to draw sustenance and flourish amidst planetary waters, soils, atmosphere, and other living beings inhabiting them. The ability to engage the natural world as source of nutrition, to respond to it through all the sensory functions of the body, constructing meaning through the processes of emotional sensibility, imagination, and ideation are the psychophysical and conceptual endowments of the human gene. But beyond these fundamental behavioral capacities, a singular feature of the human genetic code is its instruction to develop transgenetic cultural codes whereby the human further invents and shapes itself in the array of languages, family and community formations, educational processes, exchange and economic systems, legal and governance structures, as well as religious symbolic and ritual expressions.

If these cultural codes have afforded the human a creative framework for an essential self-definition and self-understanding among the diverse bioregional expressions of its pan-global presence, the complex and varying arrangements of religious, educational, commercial, and legal constructs are not without ambiguity. For, even as they respond to the directives of the gene and its primordial origin from within Earth, these cultural codes have the tendency to remove the human from an intimate immediacy with the planetary body.

Caught up in the interests and exigencies of its own intraspecies affairs, the enculturated human lives at that much distance from Earth. Over time, that psychic remove became ever more pronounced as scientific understanding and its technological applications gained in ascendancy. Incrementally, every advance in power over the natural world inflated human self-regard even as it loosened the bonds of intimacy with Earth, rendered steadily more vulnerable to progressively more virulent exploitation by an increasingly commercial-industrial-consumptive human whose cultural codes long capitulated to its sway.

> Our entire industrial system can be considered as an effort to escape from the constraints of the natural world. We have created an artificial context for our existence through mechanical invention and the extravagant use of energy. In this process we have so violated the norms of limitation [that] . . . we no longer live within the organic, ever renewing world that is the natural context of our existence. (93)

Yet it is precisely their authentic viability and creativity from within the foundational wisdom of the gene that now awakens religion, education, economics, and law to Earth's devastation and their own perilous capture. "However resistant to the restraints inherent in their nature," insists Berry, "humans in the natural order of things belong to, are possessed by, and are subject to the geographical place where they reside" (93–94). Responding to the bioregional particularities and disciplines of the waters, soil, atmosphere, flora, and fauna that Earth extends in the respective places of their residence, humans may yet renew our fourfold cultural code by celebrating the sanctity, attending the wisdom, funding the renewable energies, and protecting the integrity of that which, even now, so firmly holds us.

9

Reflections on "Ethics and Ecology"

In mid-September 2021, when roughly half of the continental United States was severely parched or aflame and the other half flooded or sodden, climate catastrophe pressed in from the abstract and the future. Undoubtedly, its presence and worsened threats informed that month's earlier announcement of federal policy to quicken the pace and percentage of reliance on solar and wind energies to replace the continuing devastation of a carbon-burning economy. So, too, did climate demise finally dictate the decision by Harvard, the world's wealthiest university, to divest itself of all holdings in the fossil-fuel industry. But if those indications from governmental and educational institutions to engage principled deliberations to forestall a dangerously overheating world are heartening, there remains a question about their protracted response to harm about which evidence was known some fifty years ago. The same reservation may be held of the entire range of human cultural processes.

From its first emergence and throughout its historical development as a social species, the human has shaped and consolidated its identity and coherence, ratifying its meaning and purpose, conserving its ordered stability and consistency through the delineation of values and norms guiding decisions both quotidian and exceptional. Across familial, clan, tribal, state, and national configurations, human capacity for broadly ethical deliberation and determination, while varying in complexity and application, is an essential and long-settled feature of human thought.

As ethical consideration has become a deeply habituated resource, well exercised for the clarification of problematic concerns seeking resolution, its focus, at least in the Western tradition, has remained within an exclusively human horizon. Humans have been so intensely centered on our own intraspecies concerns that ethical sensibility toward the natural world progressively atrophied, even as that world's jeopardy became ever more apparent. Microphase human concerns continued to vigorously engage ethical discourse but with mute responsiveness to the macrophase enormity of planetary destruction. Suicide, homicide, and genocide were accorded an appropriate ethical consideration, but biocide and geocide were beyond the pale of conceptualization and found no parlance in the moral lexicon of anthropocentrism.

> We find ourselves ethically destitute just when, for the first time, we are faced with ultimacy, the irreversible closing down of Earth's functioning in its major life systems. Our ethical traditions ... collapse entirely when confronted with biocide, the extinction of the vulnerable life systems of the Earth, and geocide, the devastation of the Earth itself. We have a radically new *problematique*. (104)

But if intense self-absorption in the profusion of its microphase concerns has left the contemporary human morally insensitive and ethically speechless before the macrophase immensity of Earth's harm, its institutional tardiness and necessary but woefully inadequate recent governmental and educational measures demand further accounting from religious and economic complicity in their failure.

In its historical elaboration, if not in its primordial inspiration, the Western Christian spiritual tradition has worked a profound ambiguity in human consciousness in its relationship to the natural world. Over time, the original Edenic sanctity and goodness of the created order, the garden of communion with the divine, was marred by the insinuation of human superiority, with a mandate to dominate and a wariness of the garden's seductive allure and failure to fully satisfy. Into that alienation and longing there arose a redemptive mystique with its expectation of release from the world's dissatisfactions, a perfected fulfillment in a whole new order of a heavenly Jerusalem. Over the centuries of its ascendancy, this millennial orientation in Western consciousness, with its attendant obligations for securing its promise, received macrophase attention in moral discourse even as concern for the fate of Earth receded to a much diminished microphase commitment.

So it was that, as religion itself reluctantly surrendered primacy in the public sphere of the seventeenth century onwards to Baconian humanism on the one hand and Cartesian mechanism on the other, inert, inanimate, and infinitely extractable Earth, lacking all ethical gravity, became progressively vulnerable to utter ruination through the commercial-industrial enterprise of the nineteenth and twentieth centuries. For the millennial discontent with the existing order of things, shorn of its originally religious aspirations, remained a powerful, however furtive, presence within the Western psyche.

With masterful craft, market capitalism of the last two centuries adroitly tapped into and skillfully manipulated human dissatisfaction and desire with the insinuation that fulfillment was as near at hand as any of the tantalizing items increasingly available for sale. With ever more sophisticated enticement and with relentless insertion into every manner of media, the mercantile juggernaut, while actively provoking insatiable desire, promised surfeit in some consumer wonderworld, to use Thomas Berry's phrasing, even as its progressive depredations of the planetary body reduced it to a ruinous waste world. To those who would raise alarm at the current climate symptoms of that failing world, their cries are utterly vacuous for a certain religious remnant, ethically compromised by their long-ago abandonment of creation care. They yet proffer some apocalyptic divine intervention to rapturously deliver the faithful from the end times of their own making.

Not the descent of the heavenly Jerusalem, but the deepest conversion of the human cultural process is the transformation here required. However mired in the microphase concerns of its long-settled anthropocentrism, the human yet has access to the immense psychic energy for the macrophase liberation and reorientation of its religious, educational, economic, and legal institutions. Having arisen as the necessary and indispensable structures for human self-understanding and self-expression from within the primordial creativity of the genetic code, their renewal comes from that very same source. Prior to any cultural formations, the genetic code of the human species is the point of our most intimate communion with Earth's waters, soils, atmosphere, and other living beings. The requisite wisdom to live within the integral body of Earth in the macrophase ethos for its healing and preservation will arise from that genetically endowed communion and from nowhere else.

10

Reflections on "The New Political Alignment"

In the course of its historical development, the human species has come to varying degrees of self-understanding through its differentiation into multiple groupings of social affiliations along familial, tribal, clan, linguistic, ethnic, regional, and national configurations. In each of these self-expressions, and consolidations among them, the human clarified certain meaning and value through the resolution of differences and tensions that might otherwise have restrained their coalescence in states of permanent isolation and fragmentation. Through differences, tensions, and resolutions, the human, from its earlier geographic extension throughout the planetary expanse, has come to a certain coordinated unification of itself around certain common concerns and values.

A notable expression of this collective capacity of the contemporary human to align itself across the otherwise disparate interests and tensions of their present constitution as sovereign, autonomous nation-states across this diversity, coalesced in the Kunming Declaration of October 13, 2021. Over one hundred countries, meeting under the auspices of the United Nations Convention on Biodiversity, addressed and adopted the principal issues summarized in the Declaration's subtitle, "Ecological Civilization: Building a Shared Future for All Life on Earth." In that very phrasing, there is critical governmental recognition that the human civilizational movement toward the future will only be possible if it is inclusive and protective of Earth's fauna and flora, currently threatened with the approaching extinction of some one million species. The enormity of that loss and the gravity of its consequences for the further unraveling of life's planetary web inform the Declaration's reiteration that the primacy of biodiversity underpins every human endeavor, including the seventeen Sustainable Development Goals already recognized by the United Nations, which include: ending poverty and hunger, providing health and inclusive education, designing safe and resilient cities, and ensuring universal decent work, among others.

Without protecting and preserving those fundamental strata of dense and richly interdependent communities of plants and animals, which, in the words of the Kunming Declaration, "support all forms of life on Earth and underpin our human and planetary health and well-being, economic growth and sustainable development," the human enterprise is severely jeopardized and simply not viable (UNBC 2020, 2). Clearly noting the subsidiary nature of economic and financial prosperity to the priority of Earth's biodiversity, the Declaration stresses

> That urgent and integrated action is needed, for transformative change, across all sectors of the economy and all parts of society, through policy coherence at all levels of government, and the realization of synergies at the national level across relevant Conventions and multilateral organizations, to shape a future path for nature and people, where biodiversity is conserved and used sustainably. (UNBC 2020, 2)

The Declaration is clear about its status as simply the framework for a demanding process wherein its signatory nations will have to substantiate in precise, measurable terms and times their more exact commitments to further prevent biodiversity loss and enhance its preservation and protection.

But, in its urgency, its orientation toward the future, and its call to radical transformation of the human in its domestic and international configurations to continue its unification and coalescence around living Earth, the Kunming Declaration might be said to approach, if not exemplify, "The New Political Alignment" of Thomas Berry's essay. Its directionality toward the realization of an "Ecological Civilization" in which the human cultural process must be subsidiary to and inclusive of the integral biosphere resonates fully with Berry's oft-repeated assertion throughout the whole of his written corpus that the human is summoned to the "Great Work" of reinventing itself at the species level, beyond its otherwise disparate linguistic, ethnic, regional, and national allegiances, as it shapes itself toward an emergent Ecozoic Era. In this era, whole new modes of institutional expression in religion, governance, law, economics, education, and the arts will be animated by an ethic of intimacy with, rather than plunderous exploitation of, the integral Earth body.

Writing over twenty years earlier, Thomas Berry advances beyond the Kunming Declaration, even while fully supportive of it, with his trenchant critique of the developer mentality in its historic manifestation within the North American experience. From the start, the settler psyche betrayed its rapacity to the once thriving communities of beaver, deer, Atlantic cod, carrier pigeons, and buffalo herds, all brought to extinction or its very near brink even as the continent's magnificent stands of all manner of trees were ruthlessly and exhaustively felled. Severely depleting the continent's once rich biodiversity, the extractive mania of the mid-nineteenth century onwards for gold and other minerals, as well as coal, petroleum, and natural gas, created unimaginable waste whose massive quantities were largely hidden by burial in land sites that quickly became toxic, dumped into streams and rivers, and ceaselessly released into an ever more carbon and gaseously saturated atmosphere. The reckless destructiveness of the commercial-industrial-developer onslaught of the natural world was matched by the cunning artfulness with which it crafted an ever wider, ever more pervasive culture of consumption whose satisfaction came with planetary demise.

> The profoundly degraded ecological situation of the present reveals a deadening or paralysis of some parts of human intelligence and also a suppression of human sensitivities. . . . In all these instances we can see a disposition towards biocide, the destruction of the life systems of the planet and geocide, the devastation of the planet itself, not only in its living creatures but in the integrity of the nonliving

processes on which the living world depends. Read the publications of the business world . . . to observe the abandonment of any discipline that would limit the moneymaking concern of our industrial society, for it is precisely by this grasping after greater wealth to sustain a "better life" that we perceive "progress." (115–16)

Nevertheless, from within this most dire condition of our own making, the human is able to retrieve and enliven our own deepest identity in communion with Earth and all its beings among whom we have been birthed and whose companionship we dare not further jeopardize. As Berry writes, "Physical degradation of the natural world is also the degradation of the interior world of the human. . . . It is to lose the wonder and majesty, the poetry, music, and spiritual exultation evoked by such awesome experience of the deep mysteries of existence. It is a loss of soul" (110–11). May the Kunming Declaration continue to broaden further political alignments and, in its simple resolve to "strengthen biodiversity for meeting the needs of people," may that inestimable value to the human soul find full and ready acceptance.

11

Reflections on "The Corporation Story"

The physical, legal, political, and psychic landscape that Thomas Berry addresses in his essay
"The Corporation Story" is one of severe degradation, protective privilege, corrupted capitulation, and
colonized consciousness. While countenancing the
contributions of corporations to human experience,
his review of their rise and dominance principally
within the North American context and their more
recent transnational extensions and operations evalu-
ates the severe costs exacted by corporate ascendance
and hegemony. "We are beginning," writes Berry,
"to ask about the real quality of life achieved, the
environmental and social costs, also about the more
lasting consequences of the so-called improvements

in human life and in the integral functioning of the natural life systems of the planet" (119).

The precursors giving legal control over vast expanses of land soon to materialize in corporate form were the original Royal Charters granted by the British Crown of the seventeenth century. These were awarded to companies and sole proprietors whose charters vested monopolistic discretion over the natural resources of the soils, waters, fauna, and flora that flourished within these extensive tracts of colonial North America. Their holders and their descendants formed a landed elite well into the founding of the postrevolutionary republic. That period, extending throughout the whole of the nineteenth century, witnessed the emergence of corporate entities primarily associated with canals and railroads as well as timber, mining, grazing, oil and petroleum drilling and pumping, and a host of subsidiary ventures. Not only were the federal and state governments crucial in the granting of the initial leases to these proliferating corporations, but they were indispensable in ceding immense millionfold acres to actively open up the middle and western regions of the continent for commercial-industrial development in the manufacturing and population centers along the Atlantic Seaboard.

At the beginning of that increasingly corporatized century, land, held and so profligately dispensed by government, became increasingly commodified and reduced to mere instrumentality of profit. That orientation became all the more pronounced as the century drew to its close.

> Progressively reverence for the sacred dimension of the natural world, even for the sense of land as a commons, which had so far survived deep in European consciousness, was further diminished. The settlers found difficulty in relating to this continent in any creative manner. Some ancient fear of the wilderness in Western civilization led either to a direct assault on the various life forms of the continent or to subjugation for some utilitarian purpose. Land was for settlement and possession. Soil was for cultivation. Forests were for timber. Rivers were for travel, for irrigation of the fields, and for power. Animals such as the wolf, the bear, and the snake were for killing. Animals such as the beaver, the deer, the rabbit, and the passenger pigeon were for the fur or the food they could provide. Fish, so abundant throughout the streams and rivers and along the shores, were for catching. North America was indeed a luxurious continent awaiting human exploitation under the title of "progress" and "development." (122–23)

The sway of that mythic conceit of mastery and domination of the natural world so fixated American consciousness that it has remained the steadfast incantation, warding off all attempts to regulate or restrain corporate excess and mesmerizing popular imagination with its vaunted promises of some artificially contrived wonder world, even as it obscures the depredations inflicted on the living one. So it was that, while corporate deployment of all manner of bribery was notorious as the nineteenth century came to a close, the corporation's more effective triumph over government control was its cunning insinuation that corporate progress was fully consistent with the constitutional recognition of governmental purpose "to promote the general welfare."

This broad, unqualified alignment of the public good of society at large with the private pursuits of corporations thinly disguised the primary beneficiaries to be investors and stockholders, not the general citizenry. Nevertheless, this late-nineteenth-century stratagem to ostensibly conflate corporate and public interests in the shared movement toward a common progress was the logic reconciling twentieth-century corporate welfare with corporate libertarianism. What enabled the corporation to make the argument that it was both the fitting recipient of government support and benefits on the one hand, and entitled to disparage and resist its directives and regulations on the other, was its status as judicially recognized personhood. In 1886, the Supreme Court ruled that the Fourteenth Amendment language that so clearly protected individual citizens applied to corporate entities as well. The Amendment reads: "No state shall make or enforce any law which shall abridge the privileges or immunities of citizens of the United States, nor shall any state deprive any person of life, liberty or property, without due process of law, nor deny to any person within its jurisdiction the equal protection of the laws."

With such privilege firmly established, corporations were emboldened to seek further constitutional rights and benefits even as they characterized government restraints on their behavior as bureaucratic infringements on their presumptive freedom. Throughout the entire course of the twentieth century and into the present, corporations have pursued their conjoint enterprise of seeking to enhance their own capital welfare and privileges as legal persons, even as they opposed regulations and constraints upon them. This dual corporate endeavor was advanced immeasurably in 2010, when a bare majority of conservative Supreme Court justices found in *Citizens United v. Federal Election Commission* that corporate entities not only enjoyed the right to engage in political speech under the First Amendment, but they might do so with unlimited financial commitment.

Consolidating ever more powerfully the notion of corporate personhood, this recklessly injudicious ruling by the Court bestowed enormous political advantage on corporations to raise and spend vast sums far in excess of individual citizens to influence and determine all manner of policies affecting people and planet that the respective corporate entity might choose to advance or suppress. That outsized corporate influence and its arrogance were on clear display when the CEOs of the four most lucrative fossil-fuel companies testified before a Congressional Oversight Committee in October 2021. During the hearings they brazenly postured their industry as corporate good citizens even as they refused all responsibility for funding some four decades of climate-change denial and skepticism. Similarly, they refused to pause ongoing and future gas and oil leases on lands and waters belonging to the public, further inflaming the planetary body and its risk of cataclysmic climate collapse. Such duplicity and malfeasance are surely one of the most shameful and deadly chapters in the corporation story.

With his concern for corporate expansiveness over society and the natural world, Thomas Berry would fully endorse, with an even broader scope, Justice John Paul Stevens in his dissenting rebuke to the majority opinion in *Citizens United*. Stevens wrote:

Although they make enormous contributions to our society, corporations are not actually members of it. They cannot vote or run for office. . . . It might also be added that corporations have no consciences, no beliefs, no feelings, no thoughts, no desires. Corporations help structure and facilitate the activities of human beings, to be sure, and their "personhood" often serves as a useful legal fiction. But they are not themselves members of "We the People" by whom and for whom our Constitution was established. (*Citizens United v. FEC*, 558 U.S. 310 [2010])

12

Reflections on "The Extractive Economy"

Having traced the roots and progressive develop-ment of a deadly human oppression over Earth and the normalcy of its paradigm of domination and control, Thomas Berry indicts it as a severe transgres-sion against the ontological covenant of the universe. Denoting a reality both sacred and fundamen-tally binding, the covenantal nature of the universe addresses the primordial Mystery whence it arises and the intrinsic integrity of its yet-unfolding expres-sions over its vastness of time and its immensity of space. Sharing a common ancestry in that first origi-native pulse of creativity some 13.8 billion years ago, the differentiated forms that emerged as the universe gave shape to itself were all in bonded intimacy with each other; all substantiated the covenantal interdependence of the universe's structural integrity.

Thus it was that the early subatomic particles in their groups of bosons, leptons, mesons, and baryons, each with its particular energy and movement, would converge in their appearance as vast clouds of hydrogen and helium atoms from whose compression, under the attractive creativity of gravity, the universe became luminous in more than two hundred billion galaxies, each a unique constellation of its own billionfold stars. Then, within the thermodynamics of the Milky Way, the universe continued its ontological covenant of remaining in intimate communion with itself even as it differentiated itself in remarkably novel self-expression.

From the imploding body of a dying giant star, the universe released titanic energy, forging in that supernova event all of the gases and elements that would eventually coalesce as the Sun and its eight orbiting bodies. Of those, it is Earth that held firm to the cosmic covenant that shaped its very structure and defined its precise movement around its solar star. Formed of the elemental matter drawn by gravity's ever-present guiding attraction, Earth emerged in that same pattern of universe self-manifestation that preceded it: the emergence of novelty from the integral, coherent interdependence of multiple prior differentiations. Thus, Earth would come alive as biosphere, come to awareness and consciousness as noosphere precisely in and through its communion with the Sun and with itself as hydrosphere, lithosphere, and atmosphere. Of this process, Thomas Berry writes:

[T]he universe . . . does not exist as a vastly extended sameness. The universe exists in highly differentiated forms of expression. So too the planet Earth exists as a highly differentiated complex of life systems. The only security of any life expression on Earth is in the diversity of the comprehensive community of life. As soon as diversity diminishes, the security for each life-form is weakened. . . . These various forms of expression are so intimately related that nothing is itself without everything else. Nothing exists in isolation. . . . These aspects of the universe constitute what I would refer to as the ontological covenant of the universe. I would also note that the planet Earth fulfills this covenant with special brilliance of expression by the manner in which its hundred-some elements are shaped into the five spheres of which it is composed. . . . Each of these is further differentiated into the innumerable forms in which each finds expression. The wonder, of course, is the bonding into a single community of existence. Especially in the realm of living beings there is an absolute inter-dependence. . . . Every animal form depends ultimately on plant forms that alone can transform the energy of the sun and the minerals of Earth into the living substance needed for life nourishment of the entire animal world, including the human community. The well-being of the soil and the plants growing there must be a primary concern for humans. To disrupt this process is to break the Covenant of Earth and to imperil life. (147–48)

That peril is now upon us in the looming catastrophe of a planetary climate collapse. Throughout the entirety of Earth's body, its surface of water and land mass overheats in temperatures that both evaporate and scorch and everywhere threaten a once-organic thriving with scarcity and extinction. If 13.8 billion years of cosmic creativity attained a magnificence on Earth over the past sixty-five million years, it did so through each species' fidelity to that covenant of interdependence. Each new expression of life, migrating into or born within an already-established community of fauna and flora, persisted and flourished, adding its differentiated distinctness to the evolving creativity of the universe, only by adherence to the limitations and demands imposed upon its behavior and functioning by the larger community of organisms in which it sought belonging.

While the human species, over the majority of its historical development, may have largely observed, conformed to, and found fulfillment among life's bioregional communities where it settled and took up residence, all trace of fidelity to the covenant of Earth was severely abrogated in these last centuries of the commercial-industrial-extractive enterprise. Multiple factors have combined in human disregard for the ultimate norm of Earth's interdependence: a feckless religious detachment; a philosophical reductionism; the deployment of mechanical, electrical, and chemical technologies of massive manipulation and disruption; a jurisprudence of exclusively human self-regard; the mercantile commodification of the natural world as mere collection of resources for consumptive human exploitation and eventual discard; and the enormous concentration of corporate power in the fossil-fuel economy of Earth's now most menacing and imminent threat.

Attention to each of these factors may identify an appropriate path forward. What is clear, however, and what even now registers its dread is the enormity of what lies ahead. A radical transformation of the collective human species presses the question of whence will come the psychic energy for such an undertaking, whence the enthusiastic resolve to counter anxiety and despair?

In June and December with their respective summer and winter solstice moments, it is Earth itself, in its fidelity to the ontological covenant of the universe from which it emerged, that is heartened for the trials of the future that has now arrived. Turning in the precise pace of its diurnal axis, with its consistent alternation of day and night, Earth simultaneously moves in its annual elliptical orbit around the Sun. In that graced passage of Earth's communion with its solar star, life blossomed and has flourished in the seasonal transitions of that great constancy. It is too awesome and stunning a movement to go unobserved and unsung, and uncounted millennia of humans past have rejoiced and been renewed in equinox and solstice observances, celebrating Earth's covenant with the Sun and knowing its journey to be their own. In this hour of darkest forgetfulness and deepest need, may the human retrieve our lost identity with and as Earth and know the psychic and physical energies that the Sun's beneficence may yet bestow.

13

Reflections on "The Petroleum Interval"

An interval may be generally understood as a period of time in which a particular condition persists. As such, it may be brief or protracted but is essentially temporary. While the end of an interval may suggest a return to the state of affairs before the interval arose—a resumption of conditions before the interval's intervention—such an assumption cannot be made of the petroleum interval within the organic creativity of Earth.

In the extraordinary brevity of its still-persistent extraction and deployment by the human industrial process, petroleum has wreaked so severe a debilitation that there can be no return to the planetary plenitude of two centuries ago, when petroleum began its fateful ascendancy. Once, it seeped naturally into comparatively modest surface pools, where it was widely used throughout a broad expanse of ancient human societies for caulking boats, sealing and waterproofing baskets, offering light and heat, and even serving for medicinal purposes. That benign phase of petroleum's history was ended with the mid-nineteenth-century technology of drilling deep into Earth's depths, there to reveal and access petroleum's vast immensity. That achievement of human ingenuity was speedily complemented by chemical and engineering skills that advanced petroleum's refined application in the increased industrial mechanization of the late nineteenth and the entirety of the twentieth century.

The invention of the internal combustion engine and the mass manufacture of automobiles are of singular and lasting impact on the extraction from petroleum's largely liquid and viscous sequestration within Earth's interior. In these engines, petroleum is transmuted and dispersed in its gaseous state into the planetary breath of Earth's atmosphere. Combined with aviation, the automotive industry quickly became and remains the commercial sector driving petroleum's saturation and perilous suffocation of the planetary body.

Additionally, petroleum has thoroughly transfigured Earth's land and water surface in the massive infrastructure of its extractive and refining processes, its extensive pipeline and rail-transport systems, and the astounding network of its concrete and asphalt configurations for the roads and highways carrying the billionfold cars that it currently fuels.

Beyond the allure of the mobility it promised, petroleum further insinuated itself in the human psyche by the ease, comfort, and well-being that its synthetic transformations afforded. By one estimate, upwards of six thousand products are petroleum derivatives, from healthcare equipment to home furnishings; medications to computer and telecommunication devices; apparel to refrigerants; eyeglasses to toothpaste; herbicides, insecticides, and fertilizer. In the profound engagement that petroleum has evoked from the human creative potential and its widespread and pervasive deployment from that venture into every aspect of physical culture, it has beguiled human consciousness in the conceit of our own technical prowess and our disregard for the well-being of the integral Earth community upon which is our ultimate dependence.

> The difficulty of the petroleum period was that the well-being of the human was the final referent as regards reality and value. We could do so many things with petroleum that we began to have illusions concerning ourselves

and our freedom to shape a world of our own that would challenge our dependence on nature. Everything on Earth, it seemed, got its value from its relation to the human. In reality the original design for Earth was for a planet that would be a triumph of diversity inter-acting with itself in a vast range of relation-ships. The well-being of each component part would be intimately related to the well-being of the other parts and to the well-being of the whole. . . . Here is where the modern indus-trial world reveals itself as failing in its larger purposes even while it seems to accomplish so much. It has failed to align its own functioning with the functioning of the planetary forces on which it depends. (156–57)

So it is that, mesmerized and inflated by our alchemical wizardry with petroleum and its deriva-tives, the human of the last century and a half has suffered a form of attention disorder. Our focus is narrowly trained on our technologic-commercial-industrial pursuits, extracting and combusting petro-leum at ever more prodigal rates with scant regard for its terrestrial and atmospheric consequences. Petro-leum's steady displacement from the safety of Earth's interior to its vaporized accumulation as carbon diox-ide, methane, nitrous oxide, and fluorinated gases has

saturated Earth's outer filament of air. Such saturation has become increasingly deadly in its overheating of the planet and the consequent climate collapse,
threatening the finely textured, exquisitely interdependent living membrane that is Earth's biosphere.

The exacting toll of massively extracted petroleum
is becoming more and more clear. This is evident in
desiccating soils, withering and flammable grasses
and vegetation, acidic and warming oceans with their
bleaching coral reefs, evaporating glaciers and melting
ice caps, magnifying and intensifying sea and aerial
storms, and a millionfold disappearance of fauna and
flora in the finality of extinction. Human limitation
to live within the severe diminishments and instabil-
ity of petroleum's still-unfolding catastrophic costs is
already apparent. This is manifest in the desperation
of whole populations turned climate refugees, and
the socioeconomic and political tensions and conflicts
foreshadowed as such mass migrations continue to
swell and surge.

In this starkness of petroleum's destructiveness,
speculation as to the exact length of its interval, mea-
sured by its final depletion from within the reserves
of its currently remaining volume, is rendered moot
by the present necessity of ending its regime. To
wait for the decades of its ultimate exhaustion is to
court disaster of unparalleled proportions that would
overwhelm and nullify the very advances that petro-

leum may have previously fashioned. The entire human endeavor would be drastically diminished and degraded in the increasing dystopia of a planetary climate collapse. There is no question of the enormous, even sacrificial, efforts required for the contemporary human to consolidate itself sufficiently at the species level and across all cultural and ideological divides to realize itself as that generation to definitively terminate petroleum's two-century interval, thus preventing its further lingering havoc and realigning humanity within the bonds of a decidedly altered, however resilient, planetary body.

As ever, the question persists of whence comes the wisdom and psychic determination for such an undertaking? Under petroleum's spell and its own vaunted mastery with its fabrications, humans may have forgotten their authentic identity. It is nevertheless Earth itself, resonating from within the depths of its genetic presence to the human, now recalling their mutual coherence and reacting in horror and alarm to what has been perpetrated. From that inherently endowed communion, Earth instructs of its own limitations and the perilous consequences of their trespass. Importantly, from that same intimacy, Earth's fidelity remains constant in the singular and incomparable fulfillment it yet extends to the human mind and heart, beyond all technical contrivance, in the stunning beauty and intricacies of its animate sensuality in colors, textures, sounds, fragrances, contours, and movements.

No less faithful is Earth's wisdom in the present exigency of humanity's resolve to end petroleum's wreckage and preserve the planetary body's deepest and cherished identity. "A person can only marvel that scientists generally seem never to have reflected on or explained to the community why the petroleum is buried in the Earth in the first place," Berry writes (158). At one time in its early unfolding, Earth creativity manifested in the sedimentary dynamics of consigning deep within itself the organic decay of algae and zooplankton bodies in their massiveness, so that their carbon sequestration would permit the chemistry of planetary atmosphere, water, and soil to further combine in the precision that would allow life's ever more abundant complexity and flourishing. That very wisdom reappears now in Earth's human modality, as it crafts and deploys the solar, wind, geothermal, and tidal energy systems, complemented by reforestation, agriculture, and animal husbandry practices, to ensure that petroleum's deadly interval becomes, indeed, terminal.

14

Reflections on "Reinventing the Human"

Thomas Berry introduced a concise compendium of the requisites for human movement into the future by an equally trenchant expression of the fateful logic dictating their necessity and the direction for the movement's advance. Berry wrote:

> The present human situation can be described in three sentences: In the 20th century the glory of the human has become the desolation of Earth. The desolation of Earth is becoming the destiny of the human. All human institutions, professions, programs and activities must now be judged primarily by the extent to which they inhibit, ignore or foster a mutu-

> ally enhancing human-Earth relationship. (*The Christian Future and the Fate of Earth*, 117)

In the self-infatuation of our technical prowess, humans both ignored and inhibited our organic coherence with Earth. Our inextricable destiny becomes nevertheless ever more palpable in what now threatens the human from our desolation of planetary waters, soils, disappearing biota, and carbon-saturated, climatically destabilizing atmosphere. The utter failure of the civilizational process, indeed its very capture by the techno-mystique of human mastery and subjugation of the natural world, is as evident as the harms those cultural patterns perpetuate.

Religious traditions are insensitive and mutely devoid of celebrating the revelatory character of Earth as sacred community. Mercantile economics reduce and deaden the vibrant energy transactions of waters, soils, and their innumerable biota into mere fungible commodities in a global consumerist market whose pricing mechanisms severely discount or completely devalue the animate cost to Earth's vitality. Jurisprudence and legal codes are insensible to all but human harm, rendering other-than-human sentience defenseless and beyond the pale of their protections, subjugated and confined as mere property for the disposition of human possessory interests.

Educational systems are more effective in preparing students to enter the techno-commercial-industrial complex that is eroding the planetary body than in fostering within them a comprehensive understanding of Earth in the integrity of its soils, waters, atmosphere, fauna, and flora, and in cultivating the lifelong art of attending to the wisdom of Earth's tutelage and finding their deepest psychic fulfillment in preservative communion with its plenitude.

That stunted lack in the intellectual, imaginative, and emotional capacities of the contemporary human is nevertheless therapeutically addressed at the level of story. Stories are the most fundamental and accessible vehicle for reeducating and reorienting human identity that has become lost in the wayward destructiveness of our collective egocentricity. Addressing the universal receptivity to the question of origins and informed by critical reflection upon the exact precision of scientific empirical observation, the corrective story of the human emerges from within the birth of the cosmos itself some 13.8 billion years ago.

The trajectory of this immense time-developmental process is the narrative of human identity, the biography of the species.

Reinventing the human must take place *in a time-developmental context*. This constitutes what might be called the cosmological-histor-

ical dimension. . . . Our sense of who we are
and what our role is must begin where the
universe begins. Not only does our physical
shaping and our spiritual perception begin
with the origin of the universe, so too does the
formation of every being in the universe. (162)

Grounding the human within the unfolding dynamics of the cosmos is both intellectually coherent
and ethically instructive. As we humans learn of
the directionality and consistency of matter's emergence and complexification, we are simultaneously
schooled in the fundamental values present at every
phase of cosmic creativity that must now become the
guiding principles for human movement into the
future: differentiation, subjectivity, and communion.
"Our present course," Berry writes, "is a violation of
each of these three principles in their most primordial expression" (163).

As the story begins, the universe differentiated
itself into subatomic particle structures, each with
its own particularity of movement and energy from
whose interactions the universe bonded with itself
to form the further differentiations of hydrogen and
helium atoms. From these atoms' unique chemical
processes, gravity's compression furthered the cosmic tendency toward communion in the massive
incandescence of the galaxies. From within these

yet-more-novel differentiations, each distinctive in mass, rotation, and stellar composition, the universe advanced in spectacular combinations among its constitutive stars. In the Milky Way, even the shattered remnants of a supernova collapse witnessed the cosmic constancy of communion as the universe fashioned a solar system of differentiated planets in orbital concurrence around the Sun.

In its turn, the extraordinary singularity of Earth as biosphere emerged as a function of its own delineations as hydrosphere, lithosphere, and atmosphere. Then, having birthed its initial appearance on the cellular level, the universe continued its billionfold-long pattern of bonding with itself as organisms interacted with each other in ever more creative interdependencies. Each of these interdependent organisms lent its distinctive particularity to the well-being of others as, together, they responded to the possibilities and limitations of the bioregion they collectively inhabited.

The contemporary human has refused to live within those very limitations in collaborative interdependence with a communion of subjects among whose plenitude we appeared as a species and through whose abundance we have been sustained. In our refusal, we have visited Earth with such desolation that it now becomes our own fateful destiny. But if humanity is to move beyond this perilous impasse for both the planet and necessarily itself, we are unable to rely on those cultural codes that have become so problematic: those ritually bereft religious traditions, those exploitatively consumptive economic systems, those narrowly confined and highly propertized legal frameworks, and those pedagogies illiterate in the idiom of organic Earth.

As already noted, these cultural codes, while mediating self-identity to the human, have themselves become entranced and ensnared by the conceit of human superiority through technical mastery over the natural world and become complicit in its ruination. So, the human must reach beyond those dysfunctional cultural codes to reinvent itself at the species level in whole new modalities of religious, economic, legal, and educational modes of living within the planet rather than coercing the planet to live within the human.

> We need to reinvent the human at the species level because the issues we are concerned with seem to be beyond the competence of our present cultural traditions, either individually or collectively. What is needed is something beyond existing traditions to bring us back to the most fundamental aspect of the human: giving shape to ourselves. The human is at a cultural impasse. In our efforts to reduce the other-than-human components of the

planet to subservience to our Western cultural expression, we have brought the entire
set of life-systems of the planet, including the
human, to an extremely dangerous situation.
Radical new cultural forms are needed. . . . We
must find our primary source of guidance in
the inherent tendencies of our genetic coding
. . . derived from the larger community of the
Earth and eventually from the universe itself.
(160)

Returning then to its story, the universe reveals
itself to be one of astounding creativity, bringing
forth differentiated centers, with their own definitive
spontaneity, their own particular embodiment of the
wisdom that drew them forth, incorporating them
into the journey of cosmic unfoldment. For, each of
those differentiated centers had the tendency to bond
with other centers from whose communion the universe fashioned whole new orders of further differentiated creativity. While not without hazards and
setbacks, and only through dim, groping experimen-
tation over the immensity of time, the wisdom of cosmogenesis, the wisdom of the universe giving shape
to itself, remained consistent in the creative principles
of differentiation, subjectivity, and communion. From
particles, to atoms, to galaxies and solar systems,
that wisdom on Earth was the genetic guidance in

which cellular simplicity gave rise to the spectacular panorama of ever more complex life-forms, all in constant communion with bioregional soils, waters, atmosphere, and the rich communities of other plants and animals among whom they interacted as they shared their respective common habitats.

The human, in the derangement of its technocratic hubris and the errancy of its cultural codes, is in need of urgent reinvention. It will be, however, from the abiding primordial wisdom of the gene from which new biocentric religious, economic, legal, and educational norms will emerge. For it will be from that source that the human may yet retrieve itself as a differentiated center among all other living centers and rediscover its deepest fulfillment, not in their exploitation, but in their communion. That is the dream that draws us together. May our sharing further inspire and consolidate its realization.

15

Reflections on
"The Dynamics of the Future"

Threat of a dystopian future through cataclysmic climate disruption, becoming all the more
apparent in the present, is a function of human failure to heed the wisdom of an immense past. Even
as we register alarm at what might portend, humans
remain fixated within the narrowest constrictions
of a self-identity defined almost exclusively by the
technocratic mastery of the most recent centuries.
Entranced by the allure of the mechanisms in the
industrial-commercial applications that we fashion
for a market of ever more consumptive desires, the
contemporary human is abetted in those pursuits
by a myth of progress, further embedding it within
the technosphere of its present habitation. Even now,

that same mythic drive is set to intensify the culture of manipulation and mechanism by the deployment of a whole new regime of artificial intelligence.

For all its vaunted capacities to effect profound transformation within the very near future of human experience, artificial intelligence remains a highly sophisticated network of computational tools to exponentially synthesize, generate, and apply vast amounts of digital and quantum information. Upon such data, these new constructs will draw conclusions, make decisions, and initiate actions pursuant to the relevant issues of their respective application. Grave and persuasive concerns have arisen and persist concerning the direction, supervision, regulation, and managerial control over this encompassing scheme of artificial intelligence. But, even in such appropriate risk analysis and precautionary discernment, the human finds itself intensely engaged in the immediacies of its technosphere, increasingly removed from the urgencies of the biosphere of its deepest past and most secure future.

For it is solely from within that integral realm of planetary waters, soils, atmosphere, and teeming variety of flora and fauna that the human first emerged, slowly developed, and consistently derives its still-indispensable sustenance. But if Earth's vitality has nurtured the physical necessities of the human body, its plenitude of those organic forms in the array of their shapes, movements, textures, colors, sounds, and songs ever remains the beneficence to activate and expand the human psyche in the marvel and delight that they elicit.

It is not by any present artificial contrivance within its technosphere, but only from within its past emergence and continuous animation of Earth's biosphere, that the human rediscovers and retrieves those energies for a potentially viable future. Of this contrast and promise, Thomas Berry writes:

> The human venture depends absolutely on this quality of awe and reverence and joy in the Earth and all that lives and grows upon the Earth. As soon as we isolate ourselves from these currents of life and from the profound mood that these engender within us, then our basic life-satisfactions are diminished. None of our machine-made products, none of our computer-based achievements can evoke that total commitment to life from the subconscious regions of our being that is needed to sustain the Earth and carry both ourselves and the integral Earth community into the hazardous future. (166–67)

If the viable future can only be shaped by the human as grounded and identified from within the psycho-physical reality of Earth, that creativity extends to an even deeper past in the very emergence of the universe some 13.8 billion years ago. Across the immense expanse of its unfolding dynamism, the universe moved from less to more complex forms of material organization, and from less to greater modalities of awareness. In this consistent trajectory of complexity-consciousness, the universe not only reveals the proliferation and grandeur of its physical forms, but it also reveals its equally persistent capacities to recognize and reflect upon itself in those same forms.

Further specification of that broad arc of cosmic creativity identifies the threefold constants that inform the novel shaping, psychic character, and mode of interaction among those complexifying self-expressions of a universe in movement toward ever more comprehensive, ever more penetrating self-awareness. At every stage of its emergence, differentiation, self-organizing subjectivity, and communion delineate the contour and direction of cosmic becoming-toward-the-future. From early particles, through atoms, galaxies, solar systems, and planetary bodies extending to the profligacy of organic Earth, the structures of the universe remain as thoroughly distinct as their centers of organization become more and more explicit.

But if the contemporary human needs to be rigorously schooled in the wisdom of those two principles of differentiation and subjectivity, it is from within their convergence in the third principle of communion that the universe powerfully invigorates the human with the energy of celebration. This moves us beyond the alienation of our present wayward destructiveness. Throughout the expansive movement of complexity-consciousness, the cosmos drew differentiated centers of novelty through the dynamic union of similar centers from an earlier stratum of universe creativity. Particles bonded with particles to bring forth atomic structures whose combinations illuminated the universe with its hundred billionfold galaxies, each a differentiated center where numberless stars and their gaseous remnants fashioned yet new stars and their orbital planets.

With Earth, the universe deepened this pattern of communing with itself as it brought forth living cells from within the interdependence of those geologic centers of planetary waters, soils, and atmosphere. Cosmic exuberance, in and through communion, became all the more extravagant as cellular combinations over life's evolutionary development yielded prolific varieties of organisms, each in multiple interactions with others, and all in an immediacy with the integral Earth body. The consonance of communion and celebration became so established that, with the appearance of the human, the universe endowed humanity with a settled, inherent disposition to find its species fulfillment in the awe, marvel, invigoration, and gratitude that Earth's plenitude of subjects spontaneously evokes.

Human capacity for both communion and corresponding celebration among other-than-human beings, and beyond that with the cosmos as a whole, is amply attested throughout the full range of its ceremonial history. No shortage of examples may be found: from Paleolithic rudiments through finely detailed Neolithic rituals, and extending into the liturgical expressions of the various classical literate traditions. But, in the last several centuries of its industrial-commercial and progress-driven infatuation, the technohuman reduced Earth to a mere collection of inert objects and resources for consumptive exploitation. In such a diminished and barren commodification, celebration of the vital and numinous character of the cosmos articulating as Earth became more and more muted, as human remove and alienation became correspondingly more pronounced.

If there is now alarm at the devastation that has been wrought and the perilous future already arriving, that reactive terror finds no alleviation in the contrived schemes and directives of a globalized artificial intelligence network. Whatever proposals such a computational system might advance for an accelerated remediation and further protection of a severely compromised Earth, they necessarily prove insufficient. As mechanisms, however elaborately they have been crafted and will in turn craft, they elude and can never engage the deepest creativity of the universe and its wisdom vested in the human.

The singular role that only the human can fulfill and for which no artificial construct can substitute is revealed in that immense process of complexity-consciousness. For it is not only in that ever-emergent self-manifestation of ever more definite and detailed forms that the universe comes to its fullness. Correspondingly, it becomes more aware of itself as that integral plenitude whose enormity in space and extent through time realizes particular focus and acuity in the human.

It is this view of cosmic intentionality that powerfully redresses the destructive conceits of a false human exceptionalism and restores its true role in the self-recognition of the universe. In that same instruction, the cosmos, reaching beyond despair, retrieves and activates its neglected potency for celebration. From its initial primordial emergence, the universe attested so profound a creative energy, such an exuberance, that it would continue to fashion itself in the spontaneous vitality of particles, atoms, galaxies, planets, and a living Earth where the universe as human could affirm its extravagance in manifold celebration.

"The Dynamics of the Future"

The evolutionary process is neither random nor determined but creative. . . . Our main source of psychic energy in the future will depend on our ability to understand this symbol of evolution in . . . the context of an emergent universe. . . . We need to experience the sequence of evolutionary transformations as moments of grace, and also as celebration moments in our new experience of the sacred. . . . Alienation is overcome as soon as we experience the surge of energy of the source that has brought the universe through the centuries. New fields of energy become available to support the human venture. These new energies find expression and support in celebration. For in the end, the universe can only be explained in terms of celebration. It is all an exuberant expression of existence itself. (169–70)

As heir to that lineage of cosmic creativity, the humans dispose ourselves in celebration to be guided anew by a wisdom beyond any artificial contrivance for the severe ardors we must now assume. Hopeful dedication for transformed human living in the integral Earth body may yet avail in human acknowledgment and celebration of that numinous creativity of all that has preceded us and in which we are essentially immersed.

It would be philosophically unrealistic, historically inaccurate, and scientifically unwarranted to say that the human and the Earth no longer have an intimate and reciprocal emotional relationship. We are not lacking in the dynamic forces needed to create the future. We live immersed in a sea of energy beyond all comprehension. But this energy, in an ultimate sense, is ours not by domination but by invocation. (175)

16

Reflections on "The Fourfold Wisdom"

Proceeding into the future, Earth's destiny must now be guided by the collective wisdom of the human from its most ancient to its more immediate. Two sources of such guidance from a settled past to a much more recent perspective are that of Indigenous wisdom on the one hand and of observational science on the other. While highly distinctive in their temporal orientation and human responsiveness to Earth, they bear complementary insight and corrective repudiation to a dangerous discontinuity that has devastated the planetary body in its present ruination. In their complementary convergence, scientific exactitude and Indigenous sensibility identify and celebrate animate Earth far beyond its economic consignment as mere inert resource for consumptive human desire and wanton despoliation.

In its historical proximity and profound reverberations within contemporary human thought, the wisdom of science reveals the extraordinary continuity of matter. This continuity extends from its most primordial and simplest expression on the particle level through its ever more complex arrangements in galactic and planetary structures and on into the cohesive weave of Earth's lithosphere, hydrosphere, and atmosphere. Here, it manifests its wondrous appearance and ever-greater coherence among an extravagant diversity of living forms, becoming Earth's biosphere.

The wisdom of science, articulating matter's movement from the infinitesimal to the immense and from the simple to the complex, identifies the universe not as the fixity of discrete and disconnected forms. The universe is not a collection of configurations independent and autonomous one from another. Rather, the universe is the creative emergence of an integral whole whose plenitude as Earth is the extension of all that has preceded it over 13.8 billion years. Of this universe, unfolding from within itself in organic continuity through its interrelated sequence of transformations across the immensity of time, Thomas Berry writes: "Awareness that the universe is more cosmogenesis than cosmos might be the greatest change in human consciousness that has taken place since the awakening of the human mind in the Paleolithic Period" (190).

But the wisdom of science in the shift from cosmos to cosmogenesis is revolutionary not just in its conception of matter's integral coherence as it moves from simplicity to complexity. For in that very process, matter moves from lesser forms of consciousness to greater modes of consciousness. In a statically conceived universe, consciousness tended to be the sole prerogative of the human, which arrogated more and more dominance to itself in the technocratic relegation of a world of inert objects, so much resource for exploitation and discard. It is the truly revolutionary wisdom of science, in the shift from cosmos to cosmogenesis, to restore consciousness as the innate disposition of the universe. Consciousness pulses from its earliest expressions of self-organization in the particle, galactic, and planetary expressions of matter's evolutionary emergence to its more explicit modes of awareness on the cellular and more complexly arranged organisms of Earth's fauna and flora. In this revivified animation, where cosmogenesis corrects the destructive fallacy of human exceptionalism among a deadened collection of disposable objects, the universe in the body of Earth reveals itself as the communion of subjects still awaiting human acknowledgment and appropriate responsiveness. On this critical issue, the wisdom of science is relatively mute but may well be tutored by the complementary wisdom of Indigenous traditions, which never lost their intimacy and respect for the other-than-human beings, whose presence, kinship, and guidance were consistently recognized and invoked in the rich liturgical expressions of Indigenous ceremonial life.

To be specific and avoid the error of overgeneralization, one might consider the rite of "Crying for a Vision," found in the Lakota culture of the North American Plains and explained by the authoritative voice of Black Elk, with whom Thomas Berry was well versed. As in all of their principal ceremonies, this particular rite is preceded by a purification ceremony conducted in a sweat lodge whose simple circular structure represents the comprehensive inclusiveness of the entire cosmos and the full accompaniment of all beings who are formal participants with the human in every liturgical act of recognizing their communion with each other and with the Sacred Source of their shared existence. Of this symbolism and the subjectivity of all beings, Black Elk explains, as noted in a previous essay bearing repetition:

> The willows which make the frame of the sweat lodge are set up in such a way that they mark the four quarters of the universe; thus, the whole lodge is the universe in an image, and the two-legged, four-legged, and the

winged peoples, and all things of the world
are contained within it, for all these peoples
and things too must be purified before they
can send a voice to Wakan Tanka [the Great
Spirit]. (Black Elk and Brown 1953, 32)

It is significant that there may be multiple reasons for
an individual to draw aside and spend two to four
days of fasting on a secluded mountain in an intense
mode of prayer. Among them, Black Elk notes that the
individual may be of troubled mind as they antici-
pate some ordeal in the future for which they sought
resilience for its endurance. But whatever particular
reason the individual might have, there is always the
paramount intention to deepen one's psychic bond
with the community of all beings and to reaffirm
their profound kinship with the subjectivity of those
other-than-human beings as one's relatives, sharing
their own distinctive value from that common Sacred
Source from whom all things derive their origin. On
this point, Black Elk instructs:

But perhaps the most important reason for this
ritual is that it helps us to realize our oneness
with all things, to know that all things are
our relatives; and then in behalf of all things
we pray to Wakan Tanka that He may give to
us knowledge of Him who is the source of all

things, yet greater than all things. (Black Elk and Brown 1953, 46)

From its location on the mountain the ceremonial rubric continues to impress on the individual that, while physically isolated, they are far from alienated. For they are full participants in the vast cosmic community, where every being is not only their relative, but where each being has been endowed with its own wisdom and energy which offers its inspiration and guidance to those who are attentive to its communion. Of this inherent capacity for the beings of the natural world to enhance human insight and understanding into the mystery of existence, Black Elk reiterates:

All these people are important, for in their own way they are wise and can teach us two-leggeds much if we make ourselves humble before them. . . . This will help you to understand in part how it is that we regard all created beings as sacred and important, for everything has a *"wochangi"* or influence which can be given to us, through which we may gain a little more understanding if we are attentive. (Black Elk and Brown 1953, 58–59)

As we reflect with Berry's writing, we gropingly seek our footing on the shifting body that is Earth. Of necessity, we take our stance not from the splendor of some untrammeled vista, but with troubled minds and hearts at the devastation and loss of what has been wrought and the enormity of the restorative project yet ahead. In this perilous state it is nevertheless the wisdom of science and Indigenous wisdom that may clarify our vision and hearten our resolve. In its integral coherence, cosmogenesis disposes the human as the yet-unfolding expression of a universe-shaping creativity among whose communion of subjects both the human and the cosmos may yet find their mutual reciprocal fulfillment. In the Great Self of the universe, the human discovers its deepest identity and realizes its most profound purpose. Correspondingly, in the human self, the universe attains a measure of self-recognition and the celebration of itself in the fullness of its manifestations.

> The universe story is our story, individually and as the human community. In this context we can feel secure in our efforts to fulfill the Great Work before us. The guidance, the inspiration, and the energy we need is available. The accomplishment of the Great Work is the task not simply of the human community but of the entire planet Earth. Even beyond Earth it is the Great Work of the universe itself. (195)

17

Reflections on "Moments of Grace"

Amidst the sociopolitical upheaval and humanitarian devastation of international wars and their threatened intensification on the one hand, and from within the most alarming increase of domestic partisan rancor and civic alienation with its attendant cynicism on the other, we consider Thomas Berry's concluding essay in *The Great Work*.

Beyond those highly fraught conditions that fissure and roil the human species within its own consolidation, Berry probes more deeply into the norms and values of the human civilizational process and its institutions to expose their dangerous inadequacy in protecting Earth in its planetary integrity. While serving an indispensable function in human self-understanding and expression over some five millennia of their ascendancy, religion, education, law and governance, and exchange and economics in their cultural infrastructure were nevertheless mute in resisting and have been complicit in their continued silence at the depredations of Earth from the commercial-industrial technocracy of the last several centuries. Of those failed civilizational processes from across the whole of human cultures, Berry writes of both finality and promise.

> Those civilizations and cultures that have governed our sense of the sacred and established our basic norms of reality and of value and designed the life disciplines of the peoples of Earth are terminating a major phase of their historical mission. The teaching and the energy they communicate are unequal to the task of guiding and inspiring the future. They cannot guide the great work that is before us. We will never be able to function without these traditions. But these older traditions alone cannot fulfill the needs of the moment. That they have been unable to prevent and have not yet properly critiqued the present situation is evident. Something new is happening. A new vision and a new energy are coming into being. (198)

From the present moment of profound human conflict and turmoil and the even more catastrophic ongoing threat to the planetary body, Thomas Berry yet speaks of a moment of grace, even a privileged moment. This transitional moment has even now begun to unfold, bearing within itself the conditions for the further emergence of renewed creativity beyond the dangerous technocratic mindset so ruinous to Earth's flourishing. Since the central conceit of that failing destructive orientation is one of human exceptionalism and discontinuity with its exploitive domination over the natural world, grace arrives in the comprehensive story of cosmic wholeness and integrity.

From its initial plenitude, flaring forth in light and particle structures, through its subsequent transition into its incandescence as hundreds of billions of galaxies, the universe continued its transformations in the Milky Way. There it birthed from within its fullness the solar system within which Earth, in its singular turn, bore living cells. From the four-billion-year combinations of these cells, there blossomed the extraordinary array of sentient awareness in flora and fauna, including human consciousness that still marvels at, and may yet celebrate, the grace-filled lineage from which it emerged. The seamless narrative of cosmic unfolding across the immensities of space and time leaves no room for that misguided exceptionalism and pathologic disconnection in the technocratic mania of Earth's demise. Such is the grace of the universe story that it addresses the root of human alienation and begins the healing recovery of a wayward human identity and its consequent derangement. Of that salutary process, Berry writes:

> We begin to understand our human identity with all the other modes of existence that constitute with us the single universe community. The one story includes us all. We are, everyone, cousins to one another. Every being is intimately present to and immediately influencing every other being. We see quite clearly that what happens to the nonhuman happens to the human. What happens to the outer world happens to the inner world. If the outer world is diminished in its grandeur, then the emotional, imaginative, intellectual and spiritual life of the human is diminished or extinguished. Without the soaring birds . . . forests . . . streams . . . flowering fields . . . and stars at night we become impoverished in all that makes us human. (200)

But, if the grace of the universe story lies within its capacity to restore the human to its fundamental communion with all its kindred of organic Earth, thereby reorienting the human to an ethic of protection and preservation rather than exploitation and consumption, is the grace sufficient to the enormity of the task? Given the harms already inflicted, the cousin species already lost and still dwindling, and all the consequences of a planetary body severely overheating and already aflame, what of cosmic grace yet avails?

While recognition of the present gravity cannot be minimized as a powerful antidote to the inertia of prolonged cultural denial, the story of the universe further instructs and even more powerfully fortifies for the commitment ahead. The universe story attends to the manner in which it reveals its creativity throughout its long past.

In its telling, the universe manifests itself through the consistency of transitional moments in which novelty and further enhancement emerge from the finality, even the destructiveness, of previous conditions. So it is that the early particle and atomic structures, persisting in their massive clouds for the first billion years of universe unfurling, eventually collapsed upon themselves and, under the colossal compression of gravity, disappeared only to transfigure into the luminescence of those hundreds of billions of galaxies. Among them, in the Milky Way, the universe would continue to advance the conditions for further creative self-expression.

In the thermodynamics of a supernova event, the relative persistence of an immense star is an initial function of the vast quantity of hydrogen and helium burning at its core. But inevitably, as that fuel is consumed and even as the star is able to forge other elements within itself, its size steadily contracts and it is unable to resist the force of gravity, imploding on itself until its final outward explosion disperses its remaining mass into clouds of gas and whole new orders of elemental matter brought forth in that titanic shattering. Such is the graced creativity of the universe that, in the very death of immense stars, there remain the seeds for future possibilities to yet emerge.

From supernova remnants and through the ever-present shaping of gravity, the universe would constellate itself into the further contours of the Sun, among whose eight orbiting planets the grace of living Earth would blossom. But even as its cellular expression became established and the marvel of photosynthesis began to enrich the early atmosphere with the density of oxygen, that very development became toxic and killed off the majority of non-photosynthetic cells. Yet cosmic ingenuity, set within the pattern of its primordial particle emergence, on through its galactic, solar, and planetary transitions, would delineate a whole new expression of animate possibility in the form of cell structures capable of ingesting oxygen and transforming it into an entirely novel source of energy for the subsequent development and sustenance of the ever more complex life forms of yet further cosmic creativity in its Paleozoic, Mesozoic, and Cenozoic expressions.

That fundamental tendency of the universe to fashion unexpected possibility from crisis consolidated itself as life endured the severe diminishments of the five great extinctions of those first two epochs. From those catastrophic eliminations and perilous reductions among Earth's biosphere, the universe reiterated its narrative of drawing creativity from collapse. From the extinction events of the Paleozoic and Mesozoic, the universe realized an ever more prolific expression in the marvels of the Cenozoic. But, after sixty-five million years of unparalleled organic diversity, the commercial-industrial-extractive economy of the modern carbon-burning human now threatens planetary cataclysm.

In such an extremity, what of cosmic grace avails? It might be said that the universe story has already begun to heal the rupture of that pernicious exceptionalism and restore human identity within the integral coherence of Earth. Beyond that corrective instruction, the universe continues to retrieve creativity from disaster by dreaming, from within the restored human, a whole new order of dynamism and its graced availability in the solar, wind, geothermal, and tidal energies of present possibility.

Epilogue

Cosmology and Ecology: Shaping the Earth Community

This rich collection of reflections by Brian Brown casts new light on Thomas Berry's generative book *The Great Work*. Here are illuminations of Berry's integrative vision of cosmology-and-ecology as shaping the Earth community from the primal flaring forth to the present. The "Great Work," which Thomas Berry calls the contemporary role of the human, is described by Brian as a recovery of our human cosmological self within the context of our evolutionary narrative. This great self of the cosmos is also differently symbolized and celebrated in all the religions of the world. The cosmological self stands in immediate relationship with our smaller, personal self as well as all differentiated selves, the biodiversity of the Earth community. The challenge of this recovery, then, is not simply the discovery of another technology that manipulates data or information about the world. Rather, the challenge now is our entry into a journey with a fourteen-billion-year evolving universe that centers on questions about knowing who we are and what our roles are in the extinction event that we are causing. Plainly speaking, these are not simply questions that collapse any inquiry into an abstract darkness of unknowing.

Consider a philosopher of the nineteenth century, Bertrand Russell, standing at the edge of an ocean calling out for an answer and hearing only the voice of one drowning in the night. This existential sense of alienation has framed human thinking for decades, honed by an objectifying science, a metric-based economics, and religious visions of transcendent release from drowning in what is perceived as a sorrowful night of material reality. Thomas Berry realized, however, that we stand at the oceans of our planet asking again about our human journey. Now, we see that water, tides, moon, marine life are all asking of humans: What do you know of our interactions? Our evolutionary journey? Our stories?

In this book we read and learn about Thomas Berry's New Story. Brown carefully describes our emerging efforts to understand what the world has been saying to us all along. The ocean was speaking to Russell, the above-mentioned philosopher, but the "small self" of his philosophical world could not hear or comprehend the "great self" of an oceanic, interactive world. We are called from centuries of reductive thinking to recover again a sense of shaping forces in the universe that emerged in the unfolding galaxies and solar systems, and that shine forth in all the remarkable differences of the Earth community. Brian Brown's illuminations are insights into the continuity of formative cosmology, such as elements from supernovas that are still manifest in our planetary ecology. Recovering a deep affection for life, as we explore and know it, is our call to the Great Work of our times.

This is a call that was not simply muted during the centuries of colonial encounter with Indigenous peoples and with innumerable cultures of inquiry and insight. Rather, the allure of the Earth was transmuted into the commodification of land and species. This resulted in generations of injustice, exploitation, and greed that were bundled into competing goods for human consumption. Now, telling the stories of human slavery, land theft, settler colonialism, and ongoing environmental injustice seems like calling out to a drowning man in an ocean's night. Is narrating our human journey necessary in all of its terror and joy, delight and destruction? Will we acknowledge voices that have been silenced? Are there limits that inform us about a deep jurisprudence of mutuality and bonded relationality of all existence?

As we break down to break through to efficacious ways of being in the world, Thomas Berry's invitation to create a new and vibrant "Ecozoic era" emerges. We begin to see what many Indigenous and local peoples have recognized as virtues of a deeply authentic life, namely, simplicity, community, and cooperation. What Brian Brown raises up in his illuminations of Berry's Great Work are the varied implications of these interacting virtues. Like stepping stones into a future fused with our present and past, Brown's reflections illuminate Berry's contributions to rethinking deep time and mutually enhancing human–Earth relations.

John Grim
Yale Forum on Religion and Ecology

References

Berry, Thomas

  1999   *The Great Work: Our Way into the Future.*
        New York: Harmony/Bell Tower.

  2011   *The Christian Future and the Fate of Earth.*
        Maryknoll, NY: Orbis Books.

Black Elk and Joseph Epes Brown

  1953   *The Sacred Pipe: Black Elk's Account of the
        Seven Rites of the Oglala Sioux.* Norman, OK:
        University of Oklahoma Press.

Chan, Wing-tsit, comp. and trans.

  1969   *A Source Book in Chinese Philosophy.* Prince-
        ton, NJ: Princeton University Press.

IPCC (Intergovernmental Panel on Climate Change)

  2021   "Headline Statements from the Summary
        for Policymakers." *Sixth Assessment Report.*
        Geneva: IPCC Secretariat.

Olson, Paul, and Wallace Wade Miller (Thio-um-
Baska)

  1979   "The Book of the Omaha: Literature
        of the Omaha People." *Faculty Publica-
        tions—Department of English* 157. Lincoln,

NE: DigitalCommons at University of Nebraska—Lincoln.

UNBC (High-Level Segment of the UN Biodiversity Conference 2020)

2020　*Kunming Declaration: Declaration from the High-Level Segment of the UN Biodiversity Conference 2020 (Part 1) under the theme: "Ecological Civilization: Building a Shared Future for All Life on Earth" (final draft)*. Montreal: Secretariat of the Convention on Biological Diversity.